WEB FORM DESIGN
FILLING IN THE BLANKS

Luke Wroblewski

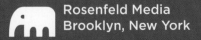
Rosenfeld Media
Brooklyn, New York

Web Form Design: Filling in the Blanks
By Luke Wroblewski

Rosenfeld Media, LLC
705 Carroll Street, #2L
Brooklyn, New York
11215 USA

On the web: www.rosenfeldmedia.com
Please send errors to: errata@rosenfeldmedia.com

Publisher: Louis Rosenfeld
Editor/Production Editor: Marta Justak
Interior Layout: Susan Honeywell
Cover Design: The Heads of State
Indexer: Nancy Guenther
Proofreader: Chuck Hutchinson

Library of Congress Control Number: 2008923241

Printed and bound in the United States of America

For everyone who has had to fill in a form.

HOW TO USE THIS BOOK

Web form design. Do we really need an entire book on such a mundane topic?

You bet we do. As arbiters of checkout, registration, and data entry, Web forms are often the lynchpins of successful Web applications.

- Checkout forms are how ecommerce vendors close deals—they stand between people and the products or services they want and between companies and their profits. For example, eBay's vast inventory (it's the 30th largest economy in the world) is driven in no small part by its Sell Your Item form.

- Registration forms are the gatekeepers to community membership— they allow people to define their identity within social applications. All of MySpace's 150+ million users joined through a Web form.

- Data input forms allow users to contribute or share information, and they allow companies to grow their content. Most of YouTube's huge video collection comes from its *Upload Your Video* form.

Web forms are often the last and most important mile in a long journey. Despite their importance, the design of forms is often poorly thought out and conceived. Your organization may have already invested heavily in opening a relationship with its customers through high-quality marketing, site design, and search engine optimization. But now it is time to "close the deal" by making sure those customers can complete your forms. And that's where this book will help.

Who Should Read this Book?

Web Form Design: Filling in the Blanks is truly for anyone who needs to design or develop Web forms—and who doesn't? Whatever type of designer you are—usability engineer, Web developer, product manager, visual designer, interaction designer, or information architect—you're probably involved in Web form design in some fashion. This book will provide you with something that you can use immediately to improve your site's forms.

If you're a beginner, you'll receive a broad overview of all the considerations that constitute good form design. If you're an experienced practitioner, you'll engage at a deeper level with issues and solutions you may not have encountered before.

What's in the Book?

This book is a collection of the insights and best practices for Web form design I've accumulated through 12 years of designing Web experiences. Wherever possible, I've conducted or referenced research to better understand the impact of Web form design decisions. Where no research was available, I've called on my own experiences and those of other designers and developers.

Just about every chapter in this book wraps up with a set of best practices that outline ways you can begin to apply the key points made within each chapter. Although these best practices can guide you toward the right design solutions for your forms, the content within each chapter explains the what, when, and why that informs each best practice.

Section One, "Form Structure," begins with an overview of why form design matters and the principles behind good form design. The remaining chapters provide a set of best practices for organizing forms and focusing people on their primary goal of completing a form.

Chapter 1: Design of Forms
Chapter 2: Form Organization
Chapter 3: Path to Completion

Section Two, "Form Elements," dives into a series of best practices for the core components that make up forms: labels, input fields, actions, and messaging (help, errors, success). Here you will find information on aligning labels, required input fields, primary versus secondary actions, automatic help systems, and much more.

Section Three, "Form Interaction," focuses on the process of filling in forms. From inline validation solutions that confirm or suggest valid answers to gradual engagement solutions that immerse people within a Web experience without forms, this section is about applying dynamic behavior to make forms more useful, usable, and enjoyable.

What Comes with the Book?

This book's companion Web site (**www.rosenfeldmedia.com/books/webforms**) contains pointers to useful Web form design articles that I've found and I've also written. It includes a calendar of my upcoming talks, and a place for you to engage in discussion with others interested in Web form design. We expect to post information on new Web form design-related resources and special discounts for related applications. You can keep up with the site by subscribing to its RSS feed (**http://feeds.rosenfeldmedia.com/webforms/**)

We've also made the book's diagrams, screenshots, and other illustrations available under a Creative Commons license for you to download and use in your own presentations. You'll find them in Flickr **(http://www.flickr. com/photos/rosenfeldmedia).**

FREQUENTLY ASKED QUESTIONS

Why does Web form design matter?

Forms enable commerce, communities, and productivity on the Web to thrive. If you are in online retail, your goal is to sell things. But standing in the way of your products and your customers is a checkout form. If you are developing social software, your goal is to grow your community. Standing in between you and community members is a form. If you've built a productivity-based Web application, forms enable key interactions that let people create and manage content. See page 4 for more information.

How should I organize my Web form—within one Web page or across several?

Who is filling the form in and why? Answering this up front allows us to think about our forms as a deliberate conversation instead of the inputs for a database. When you approach forms as a conversation, natural breaks will emerge between topics. When these distinct topics are short enough to fit into a few sections, a single Web page will probably work best to organize them. When each section begins to run long, multiple Web pages may be required to break up the conversation into meaningful, understandable topics. See page 28.

If my form spans several Web pages, do I tell people what page they're on?

When the questions that need to be answered before a Web form is complete are spread across multiple Web pages, you may want to include an overview of the number of Web pages involved (scope), an indication of what page you are on (position), and a way to save and return to your progress (status). Though closely integrated, these three progress indicators perform different functions. See page 46.

Should I top-, right-, or left-align the labels for input fields?

When you are trying to reduce completion times or if you need flexible label lengths for localization, consider top-aligned labels. When you have similar goals but vertical screen real estate constraints, consider right-aligned labels. When your form requires people to scan labels to learn what's required or to answer a few specific questions out of many, consider left-aligned labels. See page 56.

How are smart defaults used in Web forms?

Smart defaults can help people answer questions by putting default selections in place that serve the interests of most people. There are many opportunities within Web forms to utilize the power of smart defaults to reduce the number of choices people have to make and thereby expedite form completion. See page 156.

When should I include help text on my forms?

You should consider adding help text when: forms ask for unfamiliar data; people question why they are being asked for specific data; people may be concerned about the security or privacy of their data; there are recommended ways of providing data; and certain data fields are optional or required when the bulk of the form is not. See page 105.

How should I indicate required input fields?

If most of the inputs on a form are required, indicate the few that are optional. If most of the inputs on a form are optional, indicate the few that are required. When indicating what form fields are either required or optional, text is the most clear. However, the * symbol is relatively well understood to mean required. See page 75.

What's the difference between a primary and secondary action?

Actions such as Submit, Save, or Continue are intended to enable completion, which is the primary goal of just about anyone who has started filling in a form. As a result, they are often referred to as primary actions. Secondary actions, on the other hand, tend to be less utilized. See page 90.

TABLE OF CONTENTS

Form Structure

Form Elements

Form Interaction

FOREWORD

I'm sorry to break this to you, but your life is about to change.

I know this because of a study we conducted years ago when we had the opportunity to observe Master Cabinetmakers. What does building kitchen cabinets have to do with designing forms in an online application? Let me explain...

The purpose of our study was to look at the difference between those who do mediocre work and those whose work is excellent. We picked a variety of trades to study, where we could find people who were true masters. We wanted to see the differences between the masters' work and those of people whose skills weren't as refined.

This brought us to cabinetmakers. Cabinetry is a very old craft, and the people who master it are amazing in their talents and skills. They can create something that is both useful and beautiful. The best are aware their products are only a piece of the overall décor and know how to blend their results perfectly into the surrounding experience. After all, when we're in the kitchen, it's about the cooking and the family interaction—not about eternal admiration of the dovetail joints holding the utensils in place.

One of the biggest takeaways from our research was the carpenters' extreme attention to detail. Even though each person we interviewed had years of experience, nothing was taken for granted. Every hinge and joint was finely crafted, almost as if it were the most important element in their entire career. The pride they took in the final cabinet was the sum of the pride they took in each individual element.

Cabinetmakers aren't the only folks who behave this way. So are the master craftsmen of our own field, like Luke Wroblewski. In this book, Luke applies that same loving attention to detail to the design of Web forms. Like the cabinetmakers, his masterwork is both useful and beautiful. But unlike many craftsmen, Luke is willing to share his secrets outside the guildhall.

You are about to learn the secret elements of making great forms and, once you start applying this knowledge, you'll also realize that the perfection of the online experience comes from the sum of the perfect form elements and flows that go into it.

This is what will change your life: the new appreciation of how subtlety and nuance in form design can have dramatic overall effects on the total online experience (and your bottom line). And, once you learn to control those subtleties and nuances, you, too, will be a master of your craft.

As I said, your life is about to change. It starts *right ... now!*

Jared M. Spool
Founding Principal
User Interface Engineering

CHAPTER 1

The Design of Forms

Forms suck. If you don't believe me, try to find people who like filling them in. You may turn up an accountant who gets a rush when wrapping up a client's tax return or perhaps a desk clerk who loves to tidy up office payroll. But for most of us, forms are just an annoyance. What we want to do is to vote, apply for a job, buy a book online, join a group, or get a rebate back from a recent purchase. Forms just stand in our way.

It doesn't help that most forms are designed from the "inside out" instead of the "outside in."[1] Usually inside of an organization or a computer database, a specific set of information has come to define a valid record of a person, place, process, or thing. When it comes time to update or create one of these records, the organization or computer program simply says "here's the information I need," and that request shows up in front of people as a form.

For example, a Web site's database may be constructed in a way that defines a "member" as a unique combination of a first name, last name, email address, and password. So when a person tries to become a member of that site, up pops a form asking for that first name, last name, email address, and password. This is inside out. A set of database fields isn't how most people think of becoming a member of an organization or service.

Looking at things "outside in" means starting from the perspective of the people outside your organization or Web site. How would they define being a member of your service? Chances are, they'd describe it differently than your database would. They'd talk about what's on the other side of the form—for example, about the things they'd get or be empowered to do.

All this illustrates why our primary goal when designing forms needs to be getting people through them quickly and easily. Or better yet, making them invisible in a way that gets organizations the information they need and people the things they want. Forms suck. We should design accordingly.

---

[1] Lou Carbone introduced me to the terms "inside out" and "outside in" to describe how companies think about their services in a talk at MIX07: http://www.lukew.com/ff/entry.asp?532

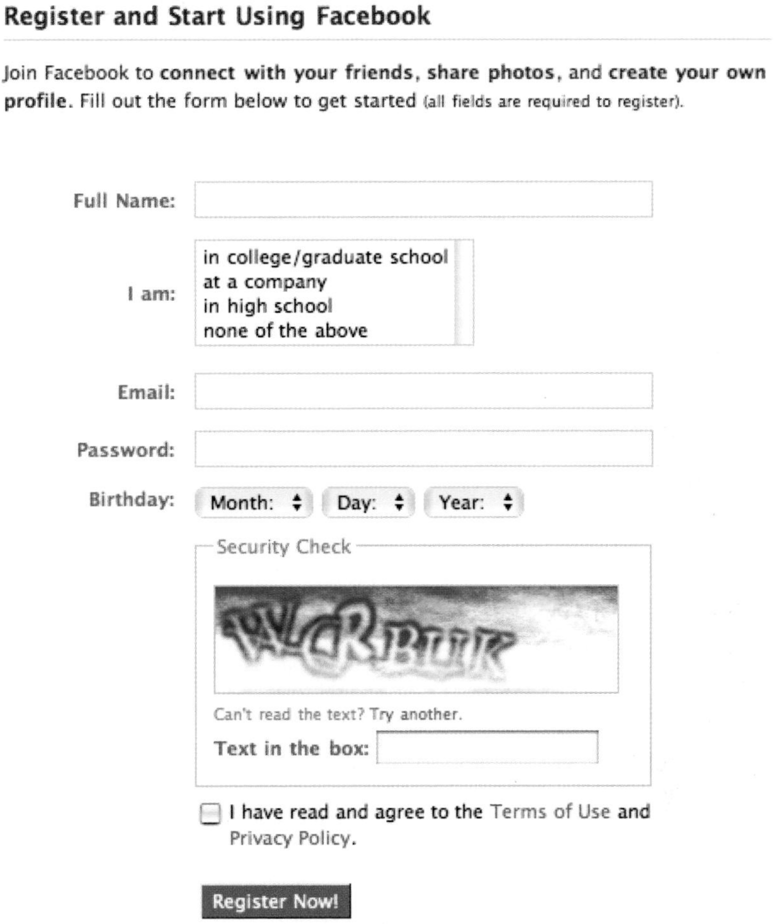

Register and Start Using Facebook

Join Facebook to **connect with your friends, share photos,** and **create your own profile.** Fill out the form below to get started (all fields are required to register).

Full Name:

I am:
in college/graduate school
at a company
in high school
none of the above

Email:

Password:

Birthday: Month: ◆ Day: ◆ Year: ◆

Security Check

Can't read the text? Try another.

Text in the box:

☐ I have read and agree to the Terms of Use and Privacy Policy.

Register Now!

FIGURE 1.1

The registration form for Facebook, a very popular social networking service. Almost half of this form is devoted to a security check!

Form Design Matters

Though knowing most people dislike filling in forms should be reason enough to care about good form design, there are plenty of other reasons why form design matters—especially online. On the Web, forms are the linchpins of ecommerce, social interactions, and most productivity-based applications.

Ecommerce

In the physical world, a typical shopping experience involves moving through product-laden aisles of colorful packaging and marketing promises. Once you select the items you need, it's off to check out where a (hopefully) friendly clerk greets you, rings up your purchases, processes your payment, bags your items, resolves any issues like missing price tags or discrepancies of cost, and bids you "good day" (see Figure 1.2).

Photograph by Andrew Walsh

FIGURE 1.2
When you're shopping in a local store, checkout usually comes with a smile.

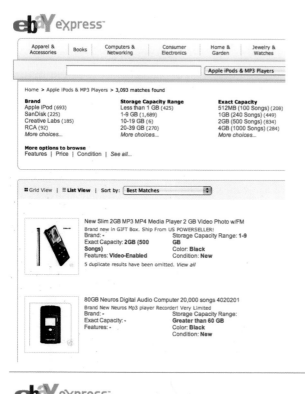

Contrast this experience with shopping online (see Figure 1.3). Within the cyber aisles of an online store, you can search and browse colorful packaging and marketing promises, stack up what you'd like in a "shopping cart," and make your way to checkout. But here the parallels end. Instead of a smiling and helpful clerk, you get a form.

The form couldn't come at a worse time. You want to buy the items you've found. The store wants to close the sale so it can make money. Standing between both your goals is a form and as we know—no one likes forms.

FIGURE 1.3
Browsing for products on the ecommerce site, eBay Express, is fun. Checking out, on the other hand, is a form.

Social Interactions

Our daily interactions with people, services, and products are enhanced through visual, tactile, and auditory cues. When having a conversation with someone, we can see their reactions and hear their voice. When we choose to engage with a group of people, the same types of interactions make us feel welcome or not.

Even physical product experiences have the same potential for engagement. Consider, for example, the initial engagement with a new Apple laptop computer (see Figure 1.4). The various materials and textures you encounter as you unwrap the packaging speak to the quality of experience you'll have with the actual computer: all the details have been well thought out. Perhaps the most personal moment comes when the computer offers to take your picture to represent your account.

FIGURE 1.4
Unpacking a new Apple MacBook Pro is a tactile, engaging experience that reflects the quality of the product inside.

However, when we're online, each of these experiences comes to us as a form. Want to join a fun new social network? Just fill in this form (see Figure 1.5). Care to share this great video with a close friend? Just fill in a form. Want to respond to an interesting author's blog post? You guessed it—a form. Just about everywhere people want to participate in social interactions online, forms get in the way. And since participation—number of members, number of activities completed, etc.—is how most social applications thrive, the organizations running these sites rely on forms for business success.

FIGURE 1.5
Vox looks like a fun social network but if you want to join, you'll need to fill out this new account form, which isn't fun at all.

Productivity

In addition to ecommerce and social interactions, the Web is increasingly a place where people get things done. From online banking to Web-based word processing, Web applications designed for productivity are growing in number. For productivity-based Web applications, the online world doesn't differ that much from the offline world. If filling in a survey in the physical world requires a form, the cyberspace version is not likely to be much different (see Figure 1.6).

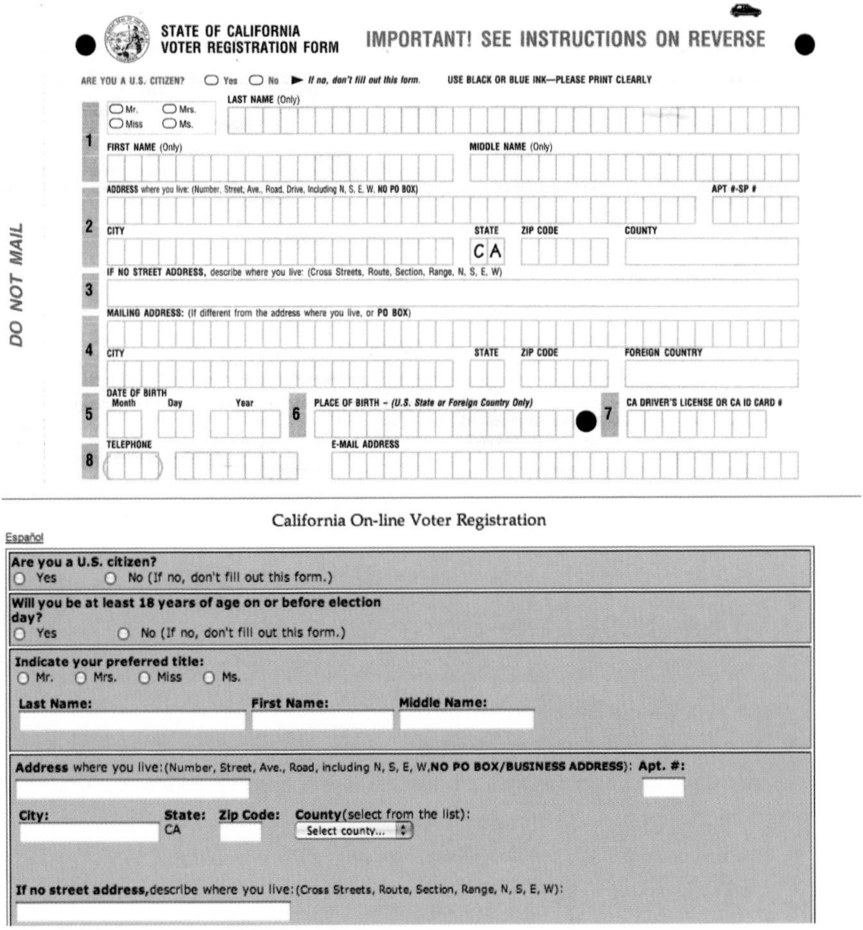

STATE OF CALIFORNIA
VOTER REGISTRATION FORM
IMPORTANT! SEE INSTRUCTIONS ON REVERSE

ARE YOU A U.S. CITIZEN? Yes No ► If no, don't fill out this form. USE BLACK OR BLUE INK—PLEASE PRINT CLEARLY

1 Mr. Mrs. Miss Ms. LAST NAME (Only)
FIRST NAME (Only) MIDDLE NAME (Only)

2 ADDRESS where you live: (Number, Street, Ave., Road, Drive, Including N, S, E, W, NO PO BOX) APT #-SP #
CITY STATE ZIP CODE COUNTY
CA

3 IF NO STREET ADDRESS, describe where you live: (Cross Streets, Route, Section, Range, N, S, E, W)

4 MAILING ADDRESS: (If different from the address where you live, or PO BOX)
CITY STATE ZIP CODE FOREIGN COUNTRY

5 DATE OF BIRTH Month Day Year
6 PLACE OF BIRTH – (U.S. State or Foreign Country Only)
7 CA DRIVER'S LICENSE OR CA ID CARD #
8 TELEPHONE E-MAIL ADDRESS

DO NOT MAIL

California On-line Voter Registration

Español

Are you a U.S. citizen?
Yes No (If no, don't fill out this form.)

Will you be at least 18 years of age on or before election day?
Yes No (If no, don't fill out this form.)

Indicate your preferred title:
Mr. Mrs. Miss Ms.
Last Name: First Name: Middle Name:

Address where you live:(Number, Street, Ave., Road, including N, S, E, W, NO PO BOX/BUSINESS ADDRESS): Apt. #:
City: State: CA Zip Code: County(select from the list): Select county...

If no street address, describe where you live: (Cross Streets, Route, Section, Range, N, S, E, W):

FIGURE 1.6
California voter registration offline and online—it's all just a form.

Yet again, we find forms standing between user needs and business goals. People want to manage their information or create new artifacts. The businesses supplying these services are interested in growing and optimizing the amount of data or customer activity they manage. The barrier for both sides is, of course, a form.

All these examples should make it pretty clear that Web forms stand in the way of user needs (what people want from a product or service) and business goals (how the organizations running these applications stay in business).

- On ecommerce sites, people want to buy the things they need and businesses want to maximize sales. Standing in the way is the checkout form.

- On social applications, people want to join communities, chat with their friends, or share content. From a business perspective, these sites want to grow and increase engagement between people. In the way are registration and contact forms.

- In Web-based productivity tools, people want to get things done and create or collaborate. Businesses want to increase the amount of content and time spent on their site. Once again, forms are in between.

So forms enable commerce, communities, and productivity on the Web to thrive. It's no wonder that form design matters.

The Impact of Form Design

Since Web forms broker crucial interactions like checkout and registration, it shouldn't come as a surprise that they can have a big impact on business goals. Increased completion rates of 10–40 percent were not uncommon in many of the form redesign projects I've been part of. And when form completion means new sales or new customers, it's easy to see how improvements in form design can amount to substantial increases in revenue (see Figure 1.7).

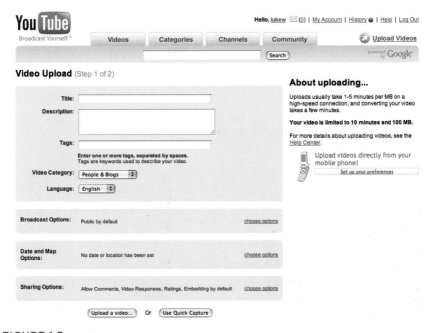

FIGURE 1.7
Where would online video sharing site YouTube be without the form that enables its customers to upload over 70,000 videos per day?

One of the biggest form redesign success stories I know of was outlined in a 2004 CHI (Computer Human Interaction) conference paper titled "A process for creating the business case for user experience projects"[2] by the eBay user experience and design team. Their registration redesign had such a positive impact on the bottom line of the company that it became a model for how design projects were evaluated and funded.

---

[2] This paper can be found at: http://portal.acm.org/citation.cfm?id=986078&dl=portal&dl=ACM

The enormous success of the eBay registration redesign was grounded in a deep understanding of the opportunities and issues present in the registration process. The team culled through usability data, customer support records, site logs, and Web conventions to inform their form redesign recommendations (see Figure 1.8).

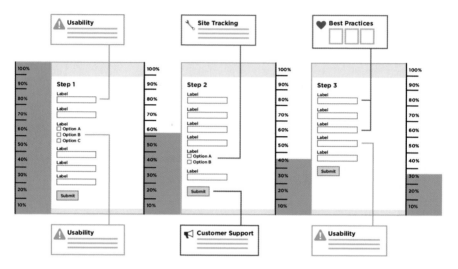

FIGURE 1.8

In the eBay registration redesign, customer support, usability findings, and site tracking data were used to illustrate major issues. The entire flow was mapped out page by page with site click-through data that illustrated user drop-off and best practice analysis.

Each of these unique sources of data provides valuable ways to measure the impact of a form design. Let's take a look at them individually:

Usability Testing: Observing how people interact with forms in a usability lab setting can provide valuable qualitative and quantitative information.

- Number and location of errors or issues

- Severity of errors or problems

- Completion rates

- Time spent to complete the form or sections of the form

- Satisfaction scores

- Subjective comments about tasks

Field Testing: Ethnographic observation of people interacting with forms in their home or office.

- Sources used to access information required by forms: documents, software, people, etc.

- Environment in which forms are filled in: loud office, small monitor, etc.

- Any additional context that informs form completion or error rates

Customer Support: Knowing the problems reported by users when filling in forms can help isolate issues and ways to resolve them.

- Top problems reported

- Common ways to resolve reported problems

- Demographic information about people reporting problems

- Operating system and Web browser settings for people reporting problems

Site Tracking: Forms can be instrumented to track any number of useful quantitative metrics.

- Completion rates

- Where people dropped off the form if they did not complete it

- How people accessed the form

- Which form elements were used

- What data was entered

- Web browser and operating system information

Eye Tracking: Recording how people make sense of the presentation of forms can illuminate points of complexity (see Figure 1.9).

- What people looked at on a form

- Number of eye fixations: level of effort required to parse a form

- Length of eye fixations: time spent looking at each element

Web Conventions: Surveying common solutions to form design problems can provide valuable insights (see Figure 1.10).

- Unique solutions to design problems

- Common patterns in use across the Web

These data points not only inform the design process, but they also help measure success. Therefore, it's a good idea to use some of these metrics with your form designs so you can better gauge your success. This doesn't

e-Commerce | Checkout Flow: Page Comparison

	Sign-in	Personal info	Item List + total	Billing Info	Shipping Info	Shipping Method	Credit Card	Other payment	Gift options	Delivery instructions	Account creation	Live help	Marketing opt-in / out	FAQ	Agree to terms	Final commit	Customer Service	Order confirmation	Trust Marketing	Sign-in	Personal info	Item List + total	Billing Info	Shipping Info	Shipping Method	Credit Card
Half	X																				X					
Land's end	X	X		X	X				X	X							X			X	O	X				X
LL Bean	X																X			X	X	X				
Macy's	X																			X				X		
Walmart	X																		X	X						
Office Depot	X	X	X	X	X		X	X			X					X						O	O	O		O
Sears		X		X	X	X			X	X												O	O	O		X
Amazon	X																				O				X	
B&N				X	X																O	X	X			X
Best Buy	X																X			X		X				
Circuit City		X															X				O				X	
Gap	X																X			X				X		
Eddie Bauer	X																			X	O	X				

X	Included on page
O	Review but not edit
X	Final commit

require a lot of expensive testing or development. Observing how a few people complete your forms or monitoring Web server logs with off-the-shelf Web analytics programs can provide a lot of useful information.

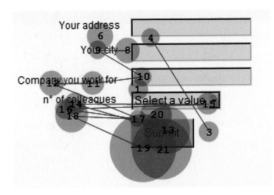

FIGURE 1.9
Eye-tracking data from Matteo Penzo's study of form label layouts published in UXmatters, July 2006, showing how people's eyes move through a simple form.

	Page 2												Page 3																		
	Other payment	Gift options	Delivery instructions	Account creation	Live help	Marketing opt-in / out	FAQ	Agree to terms	Final commit	Customer Service	Order confirmation	Trust Marketing	Sign-in	Personal info	Item List + total	Billing Info	Shipping Info	Shipping Method	Credit Card	Other payment	Gift options	Delivery instructions	Account creation	Live help	Marketing opt-in / out	FAQ	Agree to terms	Final commit	Customer Service	Order confirmation	Trust Marketing
				X																											X
	X										X	X		O		O	X	X	X					X			**X**				X
											X	X		O	O	O	X	X	X				X	X			**X**				X
			X											O			O	X					X		X						
				X	X							X		X																	
				X	X						X													X					X	X	X
	X												X											X		X					
		X									X					O	O	X						X					X		
				X													X		X					X		X					
		X													O	O	O	X		X				X		X					X

FIGURE 1.10
A Web conventions survey of online checkout forms that illuminates some interesting patterns we'll look at in a later chapter.

Perspective: Jared Spool
Founding Principal, User Interface Engineering
Changing a Button Increased Annual Revenues for a Web Site by $300 Million

It's hard to imagine a form that could be simpler: two fields, two buttons, and one link. Yet, it turns out this form was preventing customers from purchasing products from a major ecommerce site, to the tune of $300,000,000 a year. What was even worse: The designers of the site had no clue there was even a problem.

The form was simple. The fields were *Email Address* and *Password*. The buttons were *Login* and *Register*. The link was *Forgot Password*. It was the login form for the site. It's a form that users encounter all the time. How could they have problems with it?

The problem wasn't as much about the form's layout as it was about where the form lived. Users would encounter it after they filled their shopping cart with products they wanted to purchase and then pressed the *Checkout* button. It came before they could actually enter the information to pay for the product.

The team saw the form as enabling repeat customers to purchase faster. First-time purchasers wouldn't mind the extra effort of registering because, after all, they would come back for more, and they'd appreciate the expediency in subsequent purchases. Everybody wins, right?

We conducted usability tests with people who needed to buy products from the site. We asked them to bring their shopping lists, and we gave them money to make the purchases. All they needed to do was complete the purchase.

We were wrong about the first-time shoppers. They *did* mind registering. They resented having to register when they encountered the page. As one shopper told us, "I'm not here to enter into a relationship. I just want to buy something."

Some first-time shoppers couldn't remember if it was their first time, and became frustrated as each common email and password combination failed. We were surprised at how much they resisted registering.

Perspective: Jared Spool (Continued)

Without even knowing what was involved in registration, all the users who clicked on the button did so with a sense of despair. Many vocalized how the retailer only wanted their information to pester them with marketing messages they didn't want. Some imagined other nefarious purposes, such as the obvious attempt to invade their privacy. (In reality, the site asked nothing during registration that it didn't need to complete the purchase: name, shipping address, billing address, and payment information.)

Repeat customers weren't any happier. Except for a few who remembered their login information, most stumbled on the form. They couldn't remember the email address or password they had used previously. Remembering which email address they registered with was problematic—many had multiple email addresses or had changed them over the years.

When shoppers couldn't remember their email addresses and passwords, they'd attempt to guess what it could be multiple times. These guesses rarely succeeded. Some would eventually ask the site to send the password to their email address, which could be a problem if they didn't remember which email address they initially registered with.

(Later, we did an analysis of the retailer's database, only to discover 45 percent of all customers had multiple registrations in the system, some as many as 10. We also analyzed how many people requested passwords, to find out it reached about 160,000 per day. Around 75 percent of these people never even tried to complete the purchase once requested.)

The form, which was intended to make shopping easier, turned out to help only a small percentage of the customers who encountered it. (Even many of those customers weren't helped, since it took just as much effort to update any incorrect information, such as changed addresses or new credit cards.) Instead, the form just prevented sales—a lot of sales.

The designers fixed the problem easily. They took away the *Register* button. In its place, they put a Continue button with a simple message: *"You do not need to create an account to make purchases on our site. Simply click Continue to proceed to checkout. To make your future purchases even faster, you can create an account during checkout."*

The results: The number of customers purchasing went up by 45 percent. The extra purchases resulted in an extra $1.5 million the first month. For the first year, the site saw an additional $300,000,000.

On my answering machine is the message I received from the CEO of the $25 billion retailer, the first week they saw the new sales numbers from the redesigned form. It's a simple message: "Spool! You're the man!" It didn't need to be a complex message. All we did was change a button.

Design Considerations

Given the impact that form design can have on crucial metrics such as completion and error rates, it's only natural to ask: How can we design good forms? Unfortunately, the right answer is a bit unsatisfying: It depends.

It depends on the business goals, user needs, and context of your forms. It may also depend on the issues or opportunities your usability testing, live site metrics, or other data sources illuminate. In other words, there isn't just one right answer.

Fortunately, there is a way to go from the quintessential design answer of "it depends" to actionable solutions and ideas. We can do this by understanding the design considerations of the problem we are trying to solve. Design considerations are a combination of principles and patterns that provide a framework for finding appropriate solutions.

Design Principles

Design principles are the guiding light for any solution. They articulate the fundamental goals that any solution should embody. In the case of Web form design, the principles I continually strive for are

- **Minimize the Pain:** People want what lies on the other side of a form so the process of completing forms should be as simple and easy as possible.

- **Illuminate a Path to Completion:** Since the point of just about every form is to get it filled in, make it abundantly clear how people can accomplish that goal.

- **Consider the Context:** Forms rarely exist in a vacuum. They are almost always part of a broader context (audience, application, business), which informs how they'll be used.

- **Ensure Consistent Communication:** Forms broker conversations between customers and companies. Although an organization can have many groups taking part in these conversations (marketing, privacy, engineering, design, business, etc.), a form needs to speak with one voice.

Design Patterns

Design patterns, on the other hand, are actual solutions to problems in context . When applied appropriately, they enforce design principles and increase success for both user needs and business goals.

I've organized this book around the set of best practices I've come to know and utilize over 12 years of Web form design. Every best practice in the book enforces underlying principles of good form design. Most are presented as design patterns that outline how they can be applied—for example, if your goals are "x," then a good solution may be "y." Or similarly, if your constraints are "a," then a worthwhile approach is "b."

This type of structure allows you, the reader, to understand which pattern is the best practice for your particular context, so that you can go quickly from "it depends" to actionable solutions.

It's also worth pointing out that many of the best practices in this book have been informed by live-to-site, eye-tracking, and usability testing across a wide range of Web companies and users. In fact, we did some eye-tracking and completion studies just for this book. That doesn't mean we have all the right answers, but there's some real data behind these tips!

So without further ado, let's dig in.

CHAPTER 2

Form Organization

Although many visual and interaction design considerations play an important role in how people complete forms, it's often the content within the form and how we organize it that either leaves people scratching their heads or allows them to whiz through unperturbed.

What to Include

People need to parse every question you ask them, formulate their response to that question, and then enter their response into the space you have provided. The best way to speed up that process is not to ask the question at all. That means if you want to be vigilant about optimizing your forms, put every question you are asking people to the test. Do you really need to ask this question? Is it information that you can get automatically? Is there a better time or place to get an answer from people? Though this process appears tedious, you may be surprised when you discover what you can leave off your forms.

Deciding what stays on a form may mean challenging the information collected when the form was a paper document. Often, legacy questions that are no longer applicable are simply ported over when a paper form is digitized.

Agreeing as to which questions should remain on a form may also be a discussion among several departments in your company or organization. The marketing team may have specific questions to understand customers better. The engineering team may require specific information to identify unique individuals. The legal team might mandate certain terms and conditions that have to be accepted by new customers. And the list goes on.

Though all these teams may have questions they want to pose to your customers, your forms need to speak with one voice. To achieve that goal, teams will need to come together and work out which questions make it into each form. Take a look at Caroline Jarrett's "Keep, cut, postpone, and explain" framework (outlined in the sidebar) for a way to decide what makes the cut.

Perspective: Caroline Jarrett
Usability consultant, Effortmark Ltd.
Co-author: Forms That Work (Morgan Kaufmann, in press)
Co-author: User Interface Design and Evaluation (Morgan Kaufmann, 2005)
People Before Pixels

WHAT TO THINK ABOUT BEFORE YOU START

I love forms, mostly because they offer so many opportunities for improvement. And I love discussing forms with designers. So I encourage people to write to me with questions about their forms.

Often, these questions show that designers are thinking hard, which is great, but perhaps they're missing the people aspect while concentrating on pixels—the fine details, such as whether to put a colon on the end of the label. Users really don't care about colons.

USERS REALLY DO CARE ABOUT WHAT THEY'RE ASKED AND WHY

Users care about what they're asked, why they are asked it, and beyond everything else, whether those questions are appropriate to the context, meaning whatever the user is trying to achieve by filling in the form.

For example: a street address. If you have to put your street address into a Web site before browsing it, chances are that you'll react badly. Many of us maintain a convenient false set of personal answers, including an address and email that we use when we consider that it's impertinent to be asked personal questions right now.

But if you've decided on buying something that needs to be shipped, then it would be distinctly strange if the site did not ask you for a street address. And you'll probably take care to enter a real address accurately.

START BY THINKING ABOUT PEOPLE AND RELATIONSHIPS

So before you start thinking about where to place your questions on the page, think about people and relationships.

Why are users filling in your form? What is their relationship to your organization? Do they feel good or bad about it? Is this form just another stepping stone on the road to their continuing enthusiasm for your product, service, or whatever? Or is it a fearful

Perspective: Caroline Jarrett (Continued)

barrier that's keeping them from something else they'd prefer to be doing? Or are you just battling indifference: they don't care one way or another, and may just bail because they can't see the point? If you don't know enough about your users to be sure, then ask them. Watch them using your Web site or talk to them, somehow.

If you've already got questions for your form, then why are you asking those particular questions? And why are you asking them right now, at this point in the relationship? If you don't know enough about your organization to be sure, then investigate. Find someone in the organization who does know. If there isn't anyone, that's telling you that maybe your whole approach needs rethinking. Is the form necessary at all?

KEEP, CUT, POSTPONE, OR EXPLAIN: FOUR STRATEGIES FOR BETTER QUESTIONS

Maybe, as with my "shipping" example, you and your users are in harmony: you're asking for answers that they are eager to give you. Well done—keep those questions and move to thinking about the details of design.

But perhaps you're asking a question that you don't *really* need *right now*. Cut: get rid of the question and help everyone. That translates to less work for you in design, less work for your users, and no long-term storage.

Or maybe it's the "right now" part: postpone asking that question until later, until the point where it moves from unnecessary or intrusive to harmonious.

Or maybe it's one of those difficult questions that your users don't want to answer: personal data, such as a phone number, or something that requires research or extra thought. But you've investigated your form, you know that there is a real value to your organization in asking these questions, and there is some important reason why you have to ask them ahead of time. Your strategy is to explain: write a very short but clear reason why you're asking. Make sure it offers a benefit to the user— for example, "Asking you this now helps us to process your order more quickly."

And if you can't think of any benefit to the user, then you'd better go back to finding out whether you really need that question because you're going to find that you lose users at that point in the form.

Perspective: Caroline Jarrett (Continued)

YOUR VIEW, MY VIEW: BALANCING USER AND BUSINESS NEEDS

Of course, there's nothing new about being told to think about your users before starting your design. My message is about balancing user needs and business needs—harder work than stressing about labels and colons, but with a much greater impact on your form design.

Like I said: People before pixels.

Have a Conversation

Because forms facilitate conversation between a person and a company or organization, it helps to think about organizing the structure of a form as a conversation. Consider the following scenario.

You encounter a stranger who asks you: "What's your name?" "What's your address?" "What's your email address?" "What's your birth date?" Before too long you, find yourself asking: "Who is this person?" "Why does he (or she) need all this information?" "Why am I telling him (or her) all this?" Quite quickly, you become uneasy and wish the stranger would tell you something about himself or herself instead of barraging you with questions. That barrage of questions is—of course—our friend, the form.

Thinking about how a form can be organized as a conversation instead of an interrogation can go a long way toward making new customers feel welcome. I still have a vivid memory of a woman who was interviewed during a field study for a major Web retailer remarking, "This site wants to know so much about me, but I know nothing about it."

Giving people the confidence to complete forms starts with how we ask them the questions required to complete a form successfully. Input fields are the elements on a form responsible for gathering people's answers to our questions. Labels are the form elements responsible for asking the questions. Whenever these two elements can act as a natural part of a meaningful conversation, people are likely to respond with answers easily and readily.

Consider the difference between the following questions from two different versions of the Yahoo! registration form, as shown in Figure 2.1.

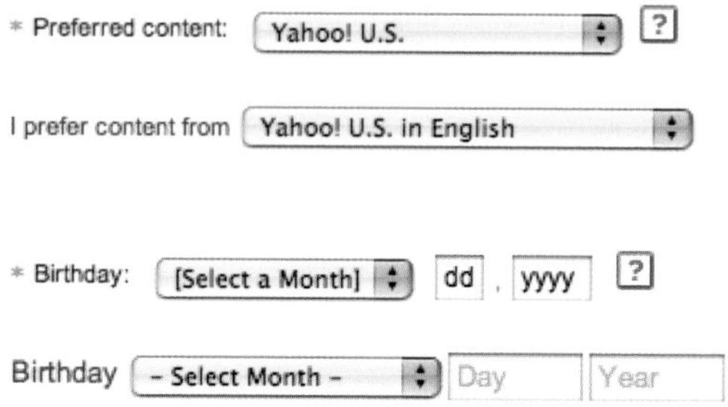

FIGURE 2.1

Two ways conversational language can clarify questions. "Day" and "Year" vs. "dd" and "yyyy"; "Preferred content" vs. "I prefer content from."

Which version seems more approachable? Which one are you more likely to have an answer for? Treating inputs as part of the question being asked (the label) mirrors the way we answer questions in the real world. This becomes even more important as the questions you ask become more complex or unfamiliar.

Consider the label "Issuing Bank." What is that asking? Now, if we rephrased it as "What bank issued you this document?" odds are that you'd have a quicker answer. Of course, both of these labels will be made clearer by their surrounding context. For example, are you filling a form about a missing financial document or a form to set up a new online account?

The terms you use in your labels also play a pivotal role in determining how quickly people can provide an answer. To continue with our banking example, do people understand the termed "issuing"? Is that vocabulary they'd use, or is it a term used by the bank? Perhaps people think instead: "Which bank gave you this document?" Using the terms your customers use to describe their actions helps frame questions in a more understandable way.

This doesn't mean that all of the labels on a form should be reworded as sentences. There are many instances when concise, single-word labels work *much* better than longer, more descriptive labels. But when there's potential ambiguity in your questions, clear conversational language often helps clear things up.

Organizing Content

In order to keep the conversation flowing smoothly, it's a good idea to organize the questions you're asking people into meaningful groups. Depending on their size and context, these groups could then be presented across multiple Web pages or as sections of a single Web page.

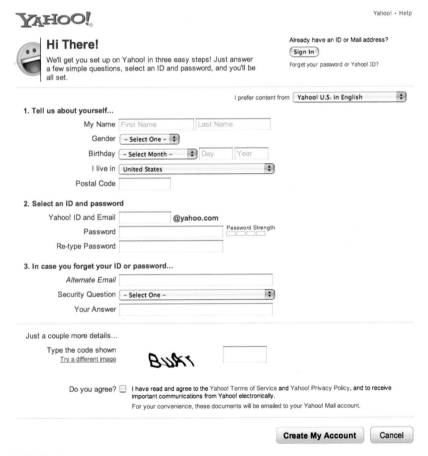

FIGURE 2.2
The new Yahoo! registration form uses a conversational tone to engage new members.

As an example, the Yahoo! registration form in Figure 2.2 groups questions about you, the account you are creating, a way for you to reaccess your account, and a few trust and safety items (terms of service and spam protection) into four distinct sections. These sections are labeled with headers that stand out from the rest of the elements on the page. The bold purple font in which they are displayed carries more visual "weight" than the other form labels, allowing you to quickly scan the form to see what type of information you'll need to provide.

Longer or more complex forms may need to distribute content groups across multiple pages, as seen in online real estate site Redfin's form for buying houses online. This overly complex process—not through any fault of Redfin—also benefits from being organized in a way that allows people to easily scan required sections they need to answer. In case someone didn't know what he was getting into when buying a home, Redfin's eight-page form makes it vividly clear (see Figure 2.3)! It's worth noting that forms this long benefit from additional feedback and interactions, which we'll discuss in later chapters.

When deciding how to organize forms, designers will often wonder if they are better off grouping all their content areas into a single Web page or dividing them into a series of pages. And if a form is divided into a series of pages, how many pages is too many? The answer, of course, is... it depends. But we can get a better answer by understanding the context for each form we design. Who is filling the form in and why? Answering this up front allows us to think about our forms as a deliberate conversation with a specific person instead of the inputs for a database.

When you approach forms as a conversation, natural breaks will emerge between topics. First, let's talk about who you are. Now let's discuss where you live. When these distinct topics are short enough to fit into a few sections, a single Web page will probably work best to organize them. When each section begins to run long, multiple Web pages may be required to break up the conversation into meaningful, understandable topics.

Other Costs (if they apply)　　　　　　　　　　　　　▸ Learn more

Who will pay the county transfer fee?
○ Buyer
○ Seller

Who will pay the city transfer fee?
○ Buyer
○ Seller

Who will pay the home owner's association transfer fee?
○ Buyer
○ Seller

Who will pay for the home owner's association transfer documents?
○ Buyer
○ Seller

Home Warranty

Do you want to order a home warranty?
[   ]

Who will pay for the home warranty?
○ Buyer
○ Seller

How much home warranty coverage?
[   ]

Which home warranty options do you want?
☐ Air conditioner　☐ Well
☐ Septic　　　　　☐ Roof
☐ Pool　　　　　　☐ Washer / Dryer / Refrigerator
Other [   ]

Liquidated Damages

Liquidated damages can be assessed if the buyer fails to complete the purchase because of default. If the buyer agrees to pay liquidated damages in case of default, then the seller retains the deposit actually paid by the buyer.

If you default, do you agree to pay liquidated damages?
○ Yes
○ No

Dispute Resolution

Rather than having disputes resolved in courts, buyers and sellers can agree to have all disputes resolved by arbitration as provided by California law.

Do you agree to submit disputes to neutral arbitration?
○ Yes
○ No

Expiration

When do you want your offer to expire? (Commonly 3 calendar days after the buyer signs and dates the offer)
[   ]

This offer shall officially expire, be deemed revoked, and the deposit shall be returned, unless the offer is signed by the seller and a copy of the offer is personally received by the buyer at 5 p.m. on the third day after this offer is signed by the buyer.

If the seller makes a counter-offer, your Redfin Agent will help you respond appropriately.

FIGURE 2.3

Redfin groups the myriad of steps required to purchase a home into a series of manageable content groups. Each section has a title and some also include a bit of descriptive text.

In certain situations, several sections with lots of questions may need to be asked in sequence because they don't make sense out of context. People need to see all the questions together in order to answer each. In this case, one long Web page may very well be the best answer.

In other situations, some sections will perform best after a form is completed. For instance, optional marketing questions such as "How did you first hear about us?" or "Would you like additional information about our services?" may actually get higher response rates when asked after someone has competed a form. In one redesign I've seen, asking these questions after a registration form was filled out increased answers by almost 40 percent! The reason behind this may be that optional questions feel less invasive when presented as follow-up topics instead of requirements for form completion.

e-Commerce | Checkout Flow: Page Comparison

	Sign-in	Personal info	Item List + total	Billing Info	Shipping Info	Shipping Method	Credit Card	Other payment	Gift options	Delivery instructions	Account creation	Live help	Marketing opt-in / out	FAQ	Agree to terms	Final commit	Customer Service	Order confirmation	Trust Marketing	Sign-in	Personal info	Item List + total	Billing Info	Shipping Info	Shipping Method	Credit Card
						Page 1																				
Half	X																			X						
Land's end	X	X			X	X			X	X									X	X	O	X				X
LL Bean	X																		X	X	X		X			
Macy's	X																			X	X				X	
Walmart	X																		X	X						
Office Depot	X	X	X	X	X		X	X		X						X					O	O	O			O
Sears		X		X	X	X		X	X												O	O	O			X
Amazon	X																				O				X	
B&N				X	X																O	X	X			X
Best Buy	X																		X	X	X					
Circuit City		X																	X	O				X		
Gap	X																		X	X					X	
Eddie Bauer	X																			X	O	X				

X	Included on page
O	Review but not edit
X	Final commit

ıse your forms aren't alone on the Web, another way to decide how
ıcture your conversations with customers is to conduct a Web
ɛntions survey to see if any patterns emerge. A Web conventions
ɛy is simply a comparison of design solutions across a number of
lar Web sites. It usually helps to look at the top performing sites in a
:ific category (like ecommerce) to ensure that the sites being compared
ɾe common measures of success.

Web conventions survey may lead you to uncover common form
ȝanization structures that have emerged on the Web. For instance,
...ıpping out what information is asked in ecommerce shopping cart forms
(see Figure 2.4) reveals some interesting insights. The first page tends to be
Sign In; the second, personal information. After that it's usually shipping
preferences. And so on.

| Page 2 | | | | | | | | | | | | Page 3 | | | | | | | | | | | | | | | | | | |
Other payment	Gift options	Delivery instructions	Account creation	Live help	Marketing opt-in / out	FAQ	Agree to terms	Final commit	Customer Service	Order confirmation	Trust Marketing	Sign-in	Personal info	Item List + total	Billing Info	Shipping Info	Shipping Method	Credit Card	Other payment	Gift options	Delivery instructions	Account creation	Live help	Marketing opt-in / out	FAQ	Agree to terms	Final commit	Customer Service	Order confirmation	Trust Marketing
			X																						X					
X							X					O		O		X	X		X			X				**X**				X
							X					O	O	O		X	X	X				X				**X**				X
		X			X							O				X						X								
			X	X							X																	X	X	X
	X							**X**														X								
X												X										X								
							X							O	O	X														
	X															X						X								
			X												X							X								X

FIGURE 2.4

In this Web conventions survey, the questions asked by 15 ecommerce checkout
forms are organized by the Web page on which they appear: page 1, page 2, and
so on.

These conventions can provide a great starting point for thinking about how to organize the conversation on your shopping cart form. Since people are likely to be familiar with these patterns, chances are they could work well in your ecommerce site. However, it's important to work from the patterns a Web conventions survey uncovers and not simply copy what the competition is doing on their site. Usually a direct replica of someone else's form organization won't be the right fit for your specific situation.

Group Distinctions

In both the Yahoo! and Redfin examples we saw earlier, each content group was visually differentiated from the rest of the form: a bold purple font on Yahoo! and a bold font and subtle background color on Redfin. As these examples illustrate, communicating meaningful distinctions between content groups doesn't require a lot of visual difference. In fact, too much contrast between content groupings often creates excessive visual noise that gets in the way of people's ability to scan a form.

Consider the differences between the following two forms in Figures 2.5 and 2.6. One relies on yellow borders, a yellow background color, red section headers, and merged table cells to group related content. The other simply relies on a subtle background color change to separate meaningful sections of the form. Using a minimum amount of visual information helps keep the focus on a form's content and not its presentation.

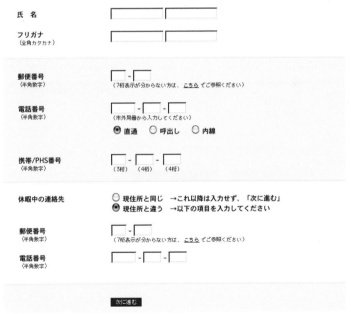

■資料送付先
⦿ 現住所に送付する
◯ その他住所（勤務先など）に送付する

■現住所以外の資料送付先住所

氏名（漢字）	氏 [　　　　]	名 [　　　　]		例）かもめ　太郎
氏名（フリガナ）	氏 [　　　　]	名 [　　　　]	（全角カタ カナ）	例）カモメ　タロウ
住所	郵便番号	[　　　　] - [　　　　]	（半角）	例）000-0000
	都道府県	選択して下さい ⬍		
	市区郡	選択して下さい ⬍		
	字丁目以降	[　　例）銀座7-3-5　　]		
	建物名	[　　　　] 例）かもめマンション203号室		
電話番号	[　] - [　] - [　]	（半角）		
FAX番号	[　] - [　] - [　]	（半角）		

◀ 戻る   ▶ 次へ

FIGURE 2.5
Many distinct visual elements on this form get in the way of seeing the questions the form is asking.

氏　名   [　　　][　　　]

フリガナ
（全角カタカナ）   [　　　][　　　]

郵便番号
（半角数字）   [　]-[　]　（7桁表示が分からない方は、こちら でご参照ください）

電話番号
（半角数字）   [　]-[　]-[　]　（市外局番から入力してください）
     ⦿ 直通　◯ 呼出し　◯ 内線

携帯/PHS番号
（半角数字）   [　]-[　]-[　]
     （3桁）　（4桁）　（4桁）

休暇中の連絡先   ◯ 現住所と同じ　→これ以降は入力せず、「次に進む」
     ⦿ 現住所と違う　→以下の項目を入力してください

郵便番号
（半角数字）   [　]-[　]　（7桁表示が分からない方は、こちら でご参照ください）

電話番号
（半角数字）   [　]-[　]-[　]

次に進む

FIGURE 2.6
A subtle background color change or thin rule is often all you need to effectively group related content in a form.

But even subtle distinctions between content groups can be overused. To account for what they consider to be shortcomings of left-aligned form labels, some designers opt to use alternating background colors to group left-aligned labels with their right-aligned inputs, as seen in Figure 2.7. However, eye-tracking studies done on label placement[1] reveal that people generally don't have problems correlating inputs to labels in a left-aligned layout (as we'll see in Chapter 4). It just takes them longer to do so. As a result, this approach doesn't really solve the problem. In fact, it can actually create a different issue.

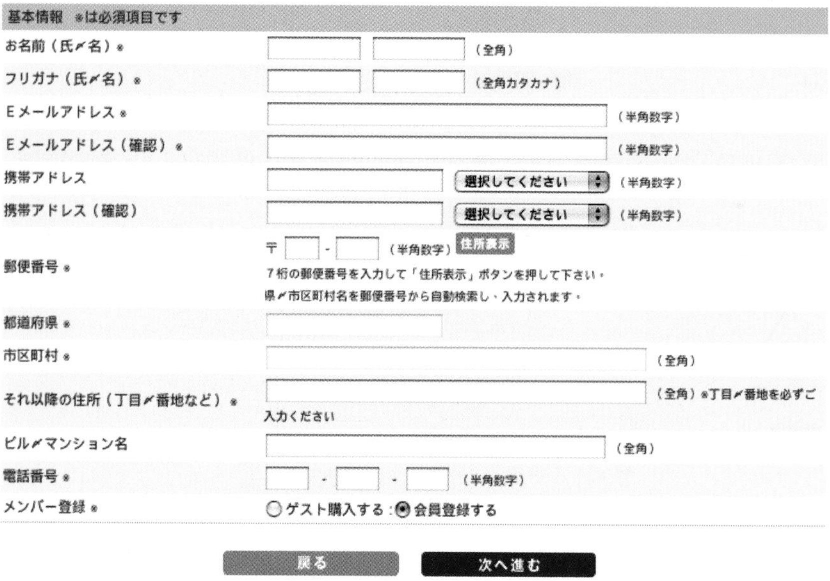

FIGURE 2.7
Although it may be tempting to use alternating background colors to group left-aligned labels and their corresponding inputs, these elements can add a lot of visual noise to a form.

---

1   Matteo Penzo's Label Placement in Forms study from UXmatters July 2006: http://tinyurl.com/fefbx

Consider the example in Figure 2.8 where two different background colors are used to distinguish labels and inputs and a horizontal rule is used to separate each label and input field pair. This approach ultimately adds an additional 15 visual elements to the layout: the centerline, each background box, and each horizontal line. These elements begin to distract our eye and make it more difficult to focus on the most important elements in the layout: the labels and inputs. As information design expert Edward Tufte points out: "Information consists of differences that make a difference."[2] In other words, any visual element that is not helping your layout ends up hurting it. This can be seen when you try to scan the left column of labels. Your eye repeatedly pauses (see the bottom of Figure 2.8) to consider each horizontal line and the box created by each combination of line and background color.

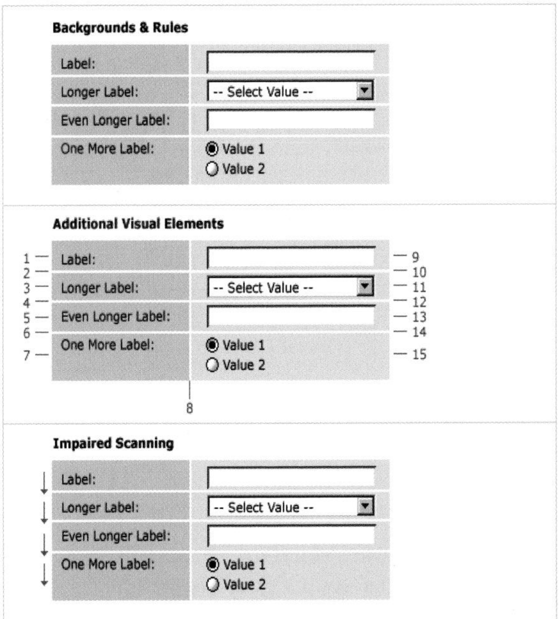

FIGURE 2.8
The addition of excessive visual elements can distract from a form's primary content: and interrupt the scan line of a form.

2   Edward Tufte, *Envisioning Information*, 1990 Graphics Press

Of course, this doesn't mean that background colors and rules should never be used within form layouts. They certainly have their place. But when thinking about how to distinguish between content groups, consider what the minimum amount of visual information needed is (see Figure 2.9). Chances are much more likely that it will become a distraction instead of an aid.

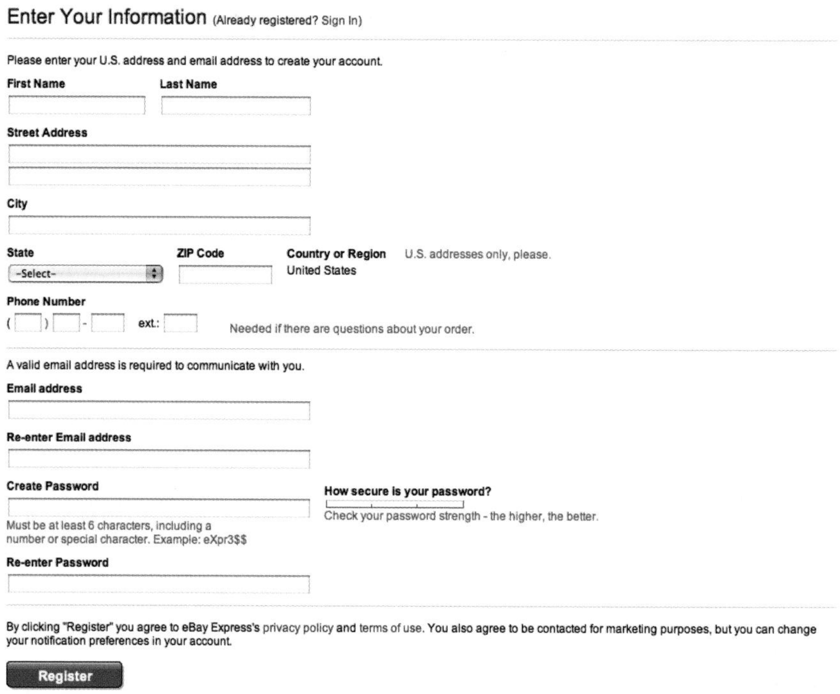

Enter Your Information (Already registered? Sign In)

Please enter your U.S. address and email address to create your account.

First Name
Last Name
Street Address
City
State
-Select-
ZIP Code
Country or Region
United States
U.S. addresses only, please.
Phone Number
( ) - ext.:
Needed if there are questions about your order.

A valid email address is required to communicate with you.

Email address
Re-enter Email address
Create Password
Must be at least 6 characters, including a number or special character. Example: eXpr3$$
How secure is your password?
Check your password strength - the higher, the better.
Re-enter Password

By clicking "Register" you agree to eBay Express's privacy policy and terms of use. You also agree to be contacted for marketing purposes, but you can change your notification preferences in your account.

Register

FIGURE 2.9

The eBay Express checkout form uses a thin rule to separate meaningful content sections. Just the minimum amount is needed to make a clear distinction.

Best Practices

- Take the time to evaluate every question you are adding to your forms. Be vigilant about removing everything that isn't necessary.

- Strive for succinctness in all the questions (labels) you ask in your forms.

- When succinct labels may be misinterpreted, look for opportunities to use natural language to clarify the questions your forms ask people to answer.

- Ensure that your forms speak with one voice, despite questions from several different people or departments.

- Organize the content on your forms into logical groups to aid scanning and completion.

- When possible, structure your forms as a conversation. Natural breaks between topics will emerge that can help you organize your form.

- If a form naturally breaks down into a few short topics, a single Web page is likely to be a good way to organize the form.

- When a form contains a large number of questions that are only related by a few topics, multiple Web pages are probably a good way to organize the form.

- When a form contains a large number of questions related to a single topic, one long Web page is generally a good way to organize the form.

- Consider asking optional questions only after a form is completed. Chances are you'll get more answers than if these questions were part of the initial form.

- Consider using Web convention surveys to discover patterns in how forms are organized on specific kinds of sites.

- Use the minimal amount of visual information necessary to distinguish content groups.

- Use initial capital letters to make the titles of content groups easier to scan.

CHAPTER 3

Path to Completion

I think it's safe to say that people should never be presented with Web forms they don't need to fill out. This, of course, means that the primary goal of anyone encountering a form is to complete it. The hope is that they want what's on the other side: to make a purchase, to start using a service, to manage information, etc. Because—I'll reiterate from Chapter 1—no one likes filling in forms. Trust me, I've asked thousands of people while talking about form design. Only one has said she enjoys it!

This means that illuminating a path to completion by showing people how they can complete a form is crucial.

Name That Form

Part of providing a clear path to completion is telling people what form they are on and what they can accomplish by filling it out. As people are unlikely to read a detailed description of what each form they encounter does, this burden mostly falls on the form's title. As a result, it's crucial that form titles match the calls to action that people use to access them.

In the Fairmont Hotels in Figure 3.1, one of the calls to action on the page is a link that allows people to "Activate Account." The form they land on after following this link, however, is titled

FIGURE 3.1

Clicking on the Activate Account link from the Fairmont Hotels front page leads to a form titled "Manage Your Fairmont President's Club Profile." Are you in the right place?

"Manage Your Fairmont President's Club Profile." Are they in the right place? Can this form be used to activate their account?

If they take the time to read the instructional text, it turns out that, in fact, they can activate their account, but these uncertainties could have been avoided altogether if the form were simply titled "Activate Your Account."

Start Pages

While the right title for a form can ensure that people start in the right place, we often have to provide some additional information on how to start. In cases where forms require a significant amount of information that people are unlikely to have readily available or a substantial amount of time to complete, start pages can provide valuable context.

When you're applying for a Fidelity account online, the start page in Figure 3.2 lets you know that account statements, a driver's license, bank account information, and more are required to successfully complete the form. You're also told the process should take around 10-15 minutes.

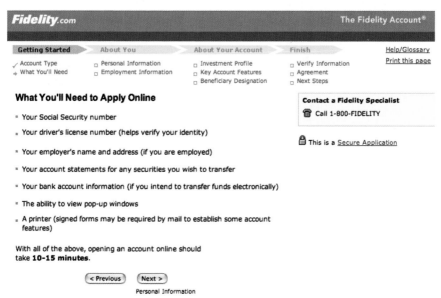

FIGURE 3.2
A start page on Fidelity lets you know what it takes to complete this form.

These types of start pages don't belong before every form—especially not on forms that ask questions you are likely to have an answer to right away. Only when forms require a significant time investment, like online surveys, or when people might get frustrated when getting halfway through a form only to discover some obscure piece of information is preventing them from finishing, should you consider using start pages to help illuminate a clear path to completion.

Clear Scan Lines

While your first inclination when thinking about illuminating a path to completion in a Web form may be to tell people where they are within a multiple Web page form, I'd like to focus first on an even more basic, but often forgotten consideration: providing a clear scan line from start to finish.

Figure 3.3 shows eye-tracking data for a simple form that highlights the importance of a clear scan line. In this example, the strong vertical axis of labels, input fields, and a primary action button provides a single path through the form. This allows people to respond quickly to questions and complete their task with a minimum number of diversions.

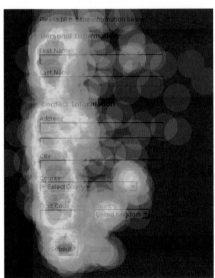

FIGURE 3.3
A composite eye-tracking image (heat map) from Etre (www.etre.com) showing what people look at when filling in a simple Web form.

To illustrate this point further, consider the difference between the two PayPal checkout forms in Figure 3.4. One has a clear scan line that starts at the first information point, ends at the primary action, and allows people to take in all the information they need to review quickly. The other has a number of different visual treatments that break up the path to completion into a series of zigzagging eye movements. A single path makes it easier to process the questions a form is asking through a consistent layout.

This, in turn, can increase completion rates by keeping people on task and ensuring that they see and respond to all the questions a form asks them.

FIGURE 3.4

Although the top form design includes some meaningful distinctions between content, the bottom PayPal form provides a clear path to completion because people can simply follow a straight line down.

A well-designed scan line has just the right amount of visual spacing between questions to enable an even pace between each label/input pair (see Figure 3.5). In other words, it allows people to move comfortably through the form without missing any important information. The right amount of spacing depends a lot on the style of your form, but generally about 50 to 75 percent of the height of an input field between each question works best.

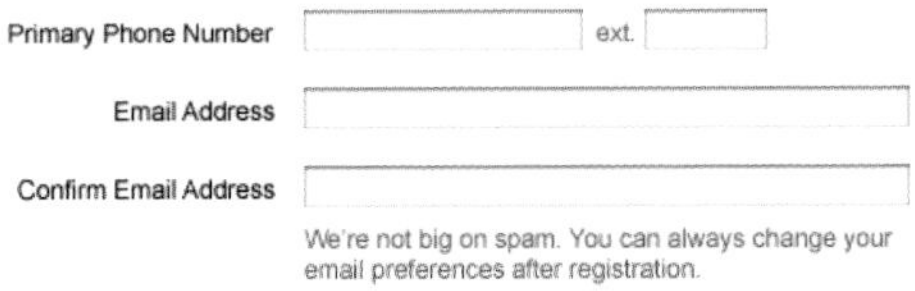

FIGURE 3.5
A well-paced flow between questions requires adequate spacing between questions.

Primary Phone Number [   ] ext. [   ]

Email Address [   ]

Confirm Email Address [   ]

We're not big on spam. You can always change your email preferences after registration.

Minimal Distractions

To keep people focused on completing a form, you also should consider which Web site elements help illuminate a clear path to completion and which elements distract from it. Even though the consistent navigation, header, or promotions that make your Web site great are appropriate on most of your site's pages, they may not be appropriate on your forms. These additional elements can be a distraction at best and a detour at worst, particularly for critical forms like checkout in ecommerce sites or registration in social applications.

Removing interface elements not directly related to completing a form helps keep people on task and removes paths to abandonment. The difference between checkout and shopping on Amazon.com shown in Figure 3.6 is stark. Even the site's logo, which usually allows people to return to the Amazon home page, is deactivated to minimize ways off this crucial form.

FIGURE 3.6

While Amazon.com may merchandise its categories and specials through its Web site, once you are in checkout, there are no frills.

Progress Indicators

When the questions that need to be answered before a Web form is complete are spread across multiple Web pages, it may be useful to communicate the status of people's progress through the form.

To illustrate this, let's return to the example of buying a house online. Years of realtors, lenders, buyers, sellers, and lawyers have added numerous clauses, considerations, and decisions to the proceedings. As a result, any form trying to enable home purchases online is going to have to account for a large quantity of required answers. The obvious first step is to organize the form into meaningful content groups. The next step is to illuminate a path to completion through these groups.

In addition to clearly labeled section headers, the Redfin form for buying a house in Figure 3.7 includes an overview of the number of Web pages involved (scope), an indication of what page you are on (position), and a way to save and return to your progress (status).

FIGURE 3.7
Redfin provides multiple progress indicators that indicate scope, position, and status information.

Though closely integrated, these three progress indicators perform different functions. The listing of the total number of pages gives people a sense of the *scope* of this form: How long will it take to complete and what are the different sections/steps? The indicator of current *position* lets people know where th[...] tive to the entire form. The form *status* indicates whether the offer w[...] ted or not and when it was last saved. For long forms, providing the[...] to save or doing so automatically is a great way to keep people on a pa[...] mpletion.

While it's certa[...] od idea to let people know how far along in a process they are[...] ed to be wary of progress indicators that incorrectly represent the numbe[...] Web pages or steps required to complete a form. An all too common practice for forms spanning multiple Web pages is the inclusion of a progress indicator that does *not* accurately mirror the number of pages a form requires.

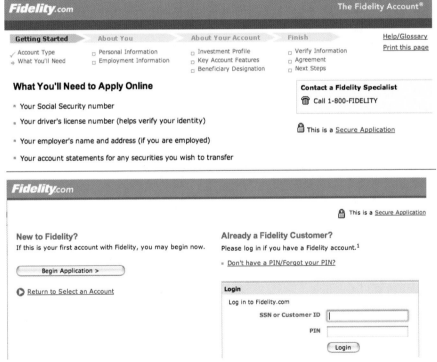

FIGURE 3.8
Fidelity.com features a two-level progress bar letting you know where you are in the process of filling in a long form. However, it disappears on step one (login), which is not included in the list of steps required.

In this Fidelity Investments example in Figure 3.8, the number of pages of inputs required to apply for an account online is outlined in a detailed progress indicator. However, as soon as someone selects "Next," a page not included in the process (Log In) appears.

This illustrates an all too common problem with progress indicators. They promise a series of well-defined, linear steps but rarely deliver. Consider a typical ecommerce checkout form like the one in Figure 3.9 on Half.com. The progress indicator states that there are three pages of inputs you can expect: shipping, billing, and place order. When it comes time to select a shipping address, however, page one is selecting from an existing list of shipping addresses. If the address you want to ship to is not listed, an additional page is required, and you need to add a new address. All of a sudden, step one becomes two steps. When selecting billing in step two, you may need to verify an online payment service provider, log in to its site, select a source of funding, or provide a new billing address. Now step two is four steps.

FIGURE 3.9
The three steps promised by Half.com can easily become many more.

So we've taken six steps to accomplish what we told our customers was going to take two steps. It's not that giving people a sense of how many steps are required is a bad thing; but we are rarely telling them the truth. One solution is to avoid the progress indicator altogether and just get people through the form as fast as possible. The other is to provide a more high-level progress indicator that does not set expectations explicitly.

The Amazon.com checkout process in Figure 3.10 makes no explicit promises about the number of steps. Instead, the progress indicator outlines the types of information you'll need to provide. Although some people could interpret these categories as separate pages, no specific expectations are set. People get a general sense of the kinds of information they'll need to provide and where they are in that process.

FIGURE 3.10
Amazon does not promise any number of pages, just a high-level set of tasks.

Perspective: Peter Wallack
Accessibility Program Director, Oracle

Designing Accessible Forms

For many disabled users, the virtual world of the computer eliminates most of the barriers of the physical world, but it's up to you, the Web page designer, to enable it. An accessible form takes into account the unique needs of users who have limited or no vision, limited or no hearing, limited physical movement, or cognitive impairments. Statistically speaking, there's a 25 percent chance that could be any one of us at some point in our lives!

Many disabled users will operate Web pages with additional hardware or software called "assistive technology" (AT), such as a screen reader or a Braille printer. It's important that you design with the proper content and structure in the first place, and then let the AT communicate with the user. Here are some areas where your design solutions that you make for accessibility purposes will benefit other users as well:

- Closed captioning of multimedia helps when you are watching TV in a noisy environment such as a restaurant, gym, or airport.

- Keyboard-only access is great for "power users," who find reaching for the mouse slows them down.

- When running over slow networks, some people disable the rendering of images, relying on the alternate text associated with those images instead.

Perspective: Peter Wallack (Continued)

One more reason to care—if you post your Web site in a public place, or if it is used by an employee of some company, or if it is sold to a government, there are probably laws that demand it be accessible.

At the heart of accessibility is usability. For example, a page that isn't usable to begin with won't stand a chance of being accessible. Think of accessibility as first requiring "uber-design":

- Uber-minimize the pain: The process of completing forms should be ridiculously easy and simple, so that someone with memory issues or attention span problems can get through it.

- Uber-illuminate a path to completion: Make it abundantly clear how people can accomplish the goal, so that a person listening to the screen can "get it" quickly without needing to hear every last character on it.

- Uber-consider the context: Some disabled users may be using sip-and-puff devices to type characters, so don't require them to type in novels!

- Uber-ensure consistent communication: A consistent presentation across all the pages makes life easier for those using a keyboard only, those using a screen reader, those with low vision, those with cognitive disabilities...everyone!

Once you adhere to these principles, the best guidelines for accessibility come from the Web Content Accessibility Guidelines (WCAG) produced by the W3C (www.w3.org/TR/WCAG10/) and the U.S. Section 508 Federal Procurement laws (www.section508.gov). Here is a brief summary of the most important accessibility requirements to consider in your forms:

- Specify text for everything that is not just fluff. This includes

    ❖ Alternative text for images (like Tooltips).

    ❖ Summary tags for tables (a brief summary of the contents of a table).

❖ Labels that are "implied" by their physical relationship to other objects. For example, address fields are often unlabeled because the relationship of address, city, state, and zip code is implied. To be accessible, each needs its own label, although that label can be hidden.

❖ Titles for frames and pages. Make them meaningful and unique.

- Make all links on a page unique, unless they really do the same thing. And give them meaningful labels that make sense out of context, as opposed to the dreaded "Click here."

- Do not use color as the only way to convey information. For example, if you color a row in a table red to indicate that something is in error, also provide a column that shows the word "Error."

- Ensure good color contrast, especially between text and backgrounds. And be aware that color-blind users cannot distinguish between certain colors. The best solution is to allow users to select colors themselves. (By the way, it's not that things are "invisible" to color-blind users; they just cannot distinguish the difference between certain colors, like red-green and blue-yellow.)

- Make font sizes large enough to read. Again, the best solution is to allow users to select their own fonts and sizes, which also means that your page has to be designed so that it scales well with large fonts, up to at least 14-point.

- Do not use gratuitous animation, as it can distract people with ADD.

- Avoid anything that flashes more than three times per second. If a user has epilepsy, this can cause an attack.

- There must be a way to accomplish all functionality on the page with the keyboard only. So if you have designed some fancy drag-and-drop interface, you must also provide a way to perform the same task without the mouse. Don't let this prevent you from doing the fancy stuff, though, since that's so much fun.

- Use clear and precise language. Also, choose your words carefully—don't refer to "the button on the right" or the "button with the green arrow." Only refer to objects by their name or function, not their physical characteristics.

- If there are timing aspects of the product, allow the user to turn them off, adjust them, or extend them. For example, if the product imposes a timeout for security or performance reasons, allow the end-user to extend it without losing any work.

- Consistency matters! Use images and text consistently across all pages of your site.

- If you convey information visually on the page by means of layout, it must also be coded that way. For example, if you show a hierarchy of data by using indentation, the same information must be available in semantic markup so that AT can interpret it. If that doesn't make any sense to you, just tell the person actually coding the page that it's his responsibility.

- Provide a way for a keyboard-only user to skip repetitive content at the top of each page. No matter how elegant you've made your navigation scheme, if you have to use the Tab key to wade through it on every page, your users will really hate you.

- Ultimately, though, there is one recommendation that dwarfs all of these: Test your page with your intended users, including those who have disabilities.

Tabbing

Every time I talk about Web form design, I always ask the audience how many of them use the Tab key on their keyboard to move between the input fields of a form they are filling out. Every time, more than half the audience raise their hands. Based on this information alone, it's a good idea to consider how people will tab between inputs to complete your form.

Consider the registration form from Office Depot in Figure 3.11. When someone is moving between input fields using the Tab key, he is likely to have a pretty jarring experience as he moves from the bottom of one column to the top of the next column. This experience would be even more disorientating in a small browser window when your last input field now sits offscreen. It also doesn't help that the first input field at the top of the second column is a single checkbox surrounded by text. This rather small input field is not that noticeable when highlighted, so a person might be a bit confused about his current position when he tabs to it. Even within the Payment Info section, the tabbing order could be unclear as he jumps between multiple rows and columns. After he specifies Payment Type, is he going to Credit Card Number next or going to Credit Card Type?

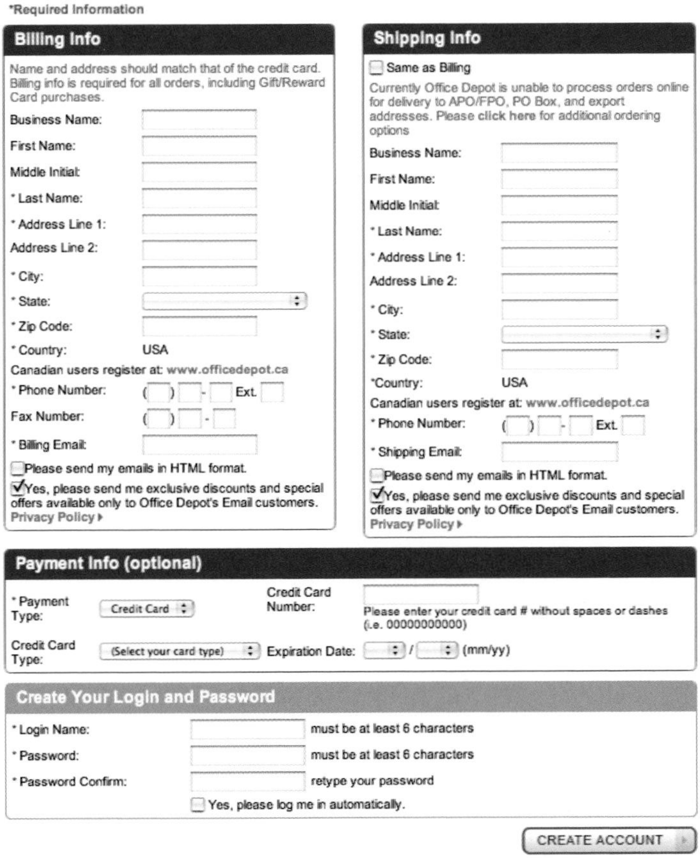

FIGURE 3.11

Tabbing through inputs on the Office Depot registration form could result in a lot of page jumping when changing columns.

By highlighting this example, I'm not saying that all two-column forms are poorly designed. However, I am pointing out that Web form designers should consider what the experience will be like for the large numbers of people who move between input fields using the Tab key, and they should design accordingly.

When I described the experience of filling out the Office Depot form previously, I assumed that the developers had specified an explicit order for the form using the "tabindex" HTML attribute. While the nuances of form development are beyond the scope of this book, it is useful for designers to know that forms that don't provide an explicit order to their inputs using tabindex will simply be tabbed through in the order they appear in the HTML markup. What that means is to avoid any existential jumps between input fields, it's a good idea to talk to a developer about specifying the order in which inputs should be accessed.

Best Practices

- Ensure that the titles of your forms match people's expectations and succinctly explain what each form is for.

- For forms requiring substantial time or information requiring look-up, use a start page to set people's expectations.

- Make sure that you illuminate a clear path to completion through a form by using clear scan lines and effective visual pacing that comfortably takes people from start to finish.

- For mission-critical forms like checkout or registration, remove distractions and any links or content that may lead to form abandonment.

- For forms with a known sequence of multiple Web pages, include progress indicators that communicate scope, status, and position.

- For forms without a clear sequence of pages, do not include progress indicators or use more general progress indicators instead of those that set incorrect expectations.

- Consider the experience of "tabbing" through a form when making form layout decisions.

- Use the "tabindex" HTML attribute to control tabbing order through a form.

Labels

E very Web form has at least three basic elements: labels, input fields, and actions. Labels are responsible for asking questions. Input fields provide a way for people to answer those questions. Actions allow people to submit the answers they have provided. While astute readers might argue that a label-less form could exist, most people would be hard-pressed to figure out how to use it.

As we saw in Chapter 2, labels need to ask people questions succinctly in a language they understand so that answering is easy. But how people answer the questions labels pose to them is also dependent on how the elements of a form are laid out.

Label Alignment

One of the most common questions asked about form design is "Should I top-, right-, or left-align the labels for input fields?" (See Figure 4.1.) So let's answer it up front. Everyone together now... "it depends." Like any design problem, the right solution depends on your specific goals and constraints.

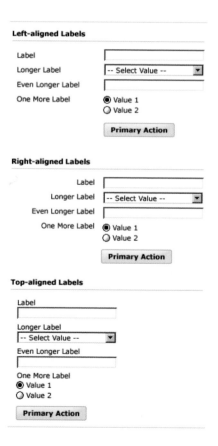

FIGURE 4.1

Left-, right-, or top-aligned labels?

You may want people to complete a form as quickly as possible and most often that's the case. Sometimes, though, you might want to slow people down so they don't make choices that aren't well thought out. Or perhaps you have screen real estate constraints that require you to minimize the amount of vertical or horizontal space your form requires. Or you may need to localize your form into multiple languages of varying lengths. The right answer between top-, left-, or right-aligned labels depends on these considerations and more.

Top-Aligned Labels

Of the three label alignment options, top-aligned labels tend to reduce form completion times the most (see Figure 4.2). Because labels and input fields are in close proximity, processing them requires little effort. Getting through the entire form is also quick and easy because people generally only need to move in one direction: down. That makes for a very clear path to completion.

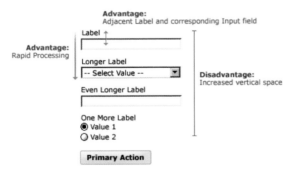

FIGURE 4.2
Some of the pros and cons of top-aligned labels.

Top-aligned labels also have plenty of horizontal real estate to expand or contract label text without negatively impacting overall page layout. This is especially useful for forms with long labels or those being localized across many cultures. Languages like French, German, or Dutch can run twice as long as English and as a result may quickly throw off a form layout.

Another advantage of top-aligned labels is that they provide a lot of horizontal space for grouping related input fields in a variety of ways, as shown in Figure 4.3. Both left- and right-aligned input labels have a lot less flexibility for these kinds of layouts, due to reduced horizontal space.

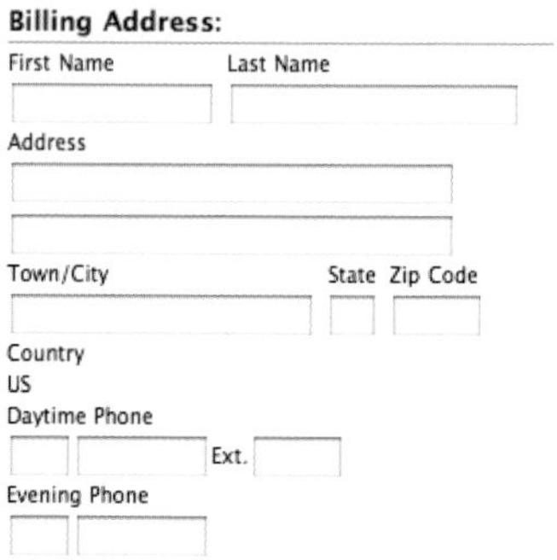

Billing Address:

First Name   Last Name

Address

Town/City   State Zip Code

Country
US
Daytime Phone   Ext.

Evening Phone

FIGURE 4.3
Top-aligned labels on Apple.com provide ample room to group related input fields horizontally.

Top-aligned labels, however, do take up additional vertical real estate. So if you're working with a small amount of vertical screen space, you might want to think twice before using top-aligned labels. It's also important to use the right amount of vertical spacing in your top-aligned layouts. Too little or too much vertical space between inputs can impede people's movement through a form. In general, it's a good idea to use 50 to 75 percent of the height of a single input field between adjacent inputs.

One of the reasons top-aligned forms are completed quickly may be because they only require a single eye fixation to take in both input label and input field. In fact, an eye-tracking study by Matteo Penzo from July 2006[1] found that moving from label to input required just 50 milliseconds (see Figure 4.4). That's 10 times faster than left-aligned labels, which required a medium duration of 500ms and twice as fast as right-aligned labels, which required up to 240ms.

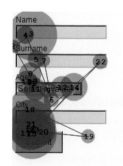

FIGURE 4.4
Eye-tracking data for top-aligned labels by Matteo Penzo.

---

[1]   *Label Placement in Forms* published in UXmatters July, 2006: http://tinyurl.com/fefbx

The results of live site testing across several different geographies have also supported top-aligned labels as the quickest way to get people through forms. These studies also had higher completion rates (over 10 percent higher) than the left-aligned versions of forms they were tested against. Because of these quick completion times and high completion rates, some designers always recommend using top-aligned labels. After all, the primary goal of any form is to get it completed with a minimum amount of pain, and the speed of top-aligned labels certainly helps.

It should be noted, however, that both the eye tracking and live-to-site testing referenced here were done with forms containing familiar data (see Figure 4.5). That means information that people generally know or can readily find such as name, address, credit card number, or email address. Whether or not these results hold up for unfamiliar data—information people have to look about or learn about—remains to be seen.

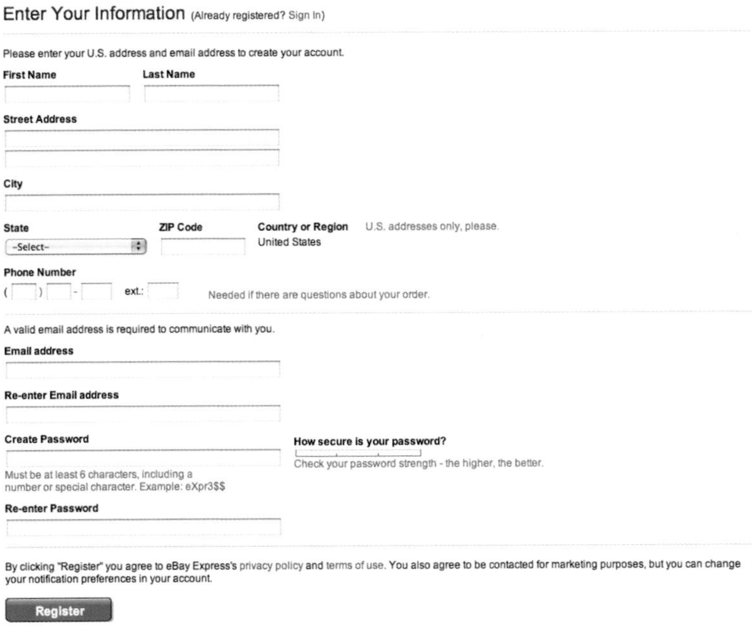

FIGURE 4.5

The eBay Express checkout form is an example of a top-aligned layout.

Right-Aligned Labels

Right-aligned labels also have the advantage of close proximity between input field and label and, as a result, are quick to complete (see Figure 4.6). The resulting left rag of the labels in a right-aligned layout, however, reduces the effectiveness of a quick scan to see what information the form requires. In the Western world, people read from left to right, so their eyes prefer a hard edge along the left side.

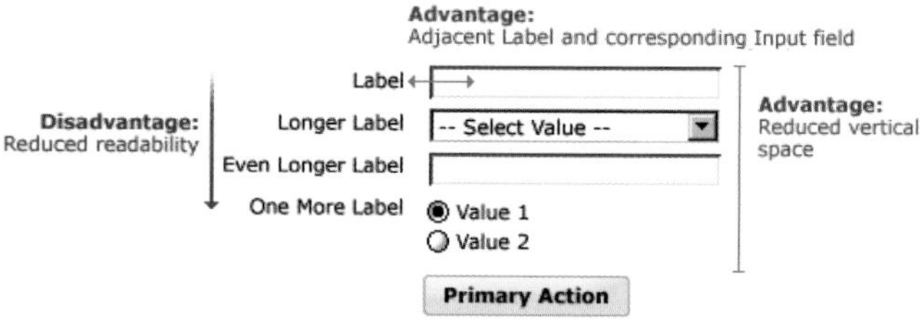

FIGURE 4.6

Some of the pros and cons of right-aligned labels.

Right-aligned labels also have flexibility issues when the label text changes widths. It's quite common to see labels wrapping to two lines of text, making scanning the form more difficult.

That said, in cases where you want to minimize the amount of vertical screen space your form uses, right-aligned labels can provide fast completion times. Matteo Penzo's eye-tracking study (shown in Figure 4.7) found that right-aligned labels required an average saccade (movement of the eyes) between input label and field of 170 milliseconds for expert users and 240ms for novices and completion times that were twice as fast as left-aligned labels. See Figure 4.8 for an example of a right-aligned layout.

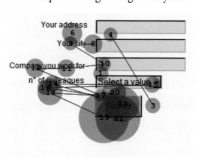

FIGURE 4.7

Eye-tracking data for right-aligned labels by Matteo Penzo.

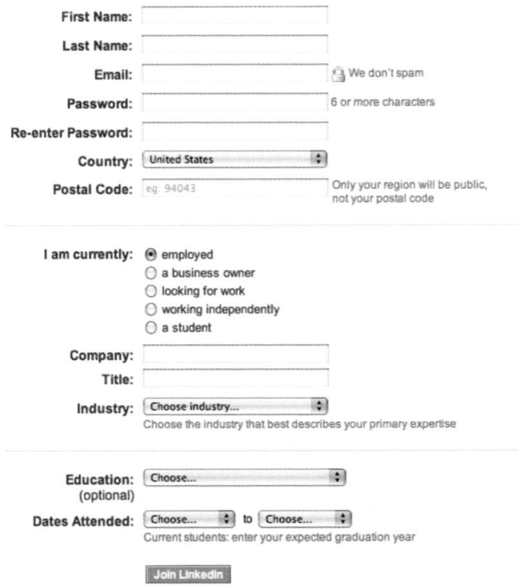

First Name:
Last Name:
Email:
We don't spam
Password:
6 or more characters
Re-enter Password:
Country:
United States
Postal Code:
eg: 94043
Only your region will be public, not your postal code
I am currently:
employed
a business owner
looking for work
working independently
a student
Company:
Title:
Industry:
Choose industry...
Choose the industry that best describes your primary expertise
Education: (optional)
Choose...
Dates Attended:
Choose...
to
Choose...
Current students: enter your expected graduation year
Join LinkedIn

FIGURE 4.8
LinkedIn's registration form is an example of a right-aligned layout.

Left-Aligned Labels

When the data being collected by a form is unfamiliar or does not fall into easy-to-process groups (such as the various parts of an address), left-aligning input field labels makes scanning the information required by a form easier (see Figure 4.9). People can simply inspect the left column of labels up and down without being interrupted by input fields.

Unfortunately, a few long labels often extend the distance between labels and inputs and, as a result, completion times may suffer. People have to "jump" from column to column in order to find the right association of input field and input label before entering data.

Disadvantage:
Adjacency of Label and corresponding Input field
Advantage:
Easy to scan labels
Label:
Longer Label:
-- Select Value --
Even Longer Label:
One More Label:
Value 1
Value 2
Primary Action
Advantage:
Reduced vertical space

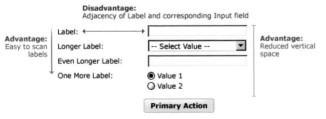

FIGURE 4.9
Some of the pros and cons of left-aligned labels.

Left-aligned labels also have the advantage of requiring less vertical screen space than top-aligned forms. However, they still carry the same disadvantages as right-aligned labels, one of which is less flexibility for label lengths and input field groupings.

The reason left-aligned forms are the slowest of the three options to complete may be because of the number of eye fixations they require to parse. People generally have no problem associating the labels in a left-aligned layout with their corresponding input fields; it just takes them a while to do so. According to Matteo's study "a medium saccade duration of 500ms (milliseconds) was typical, which is quite long, showing that users were experiencing heavy cognitive load" (see Figure 4.10).

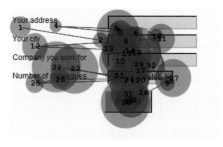

FIGURE 4.10
Eye-tracking data for left-aligned labels
by Matteo Penzo.

That said, slower completion times might not always be a bad thing. In fact, if you want people to slow down and consider each input in a form more carefully, left-aligned labels may be a good way to go, especially for forms with lots of optional fields or unfamiliar data like "Preferences" dialogs or advanced settings (see Figure 4.11).

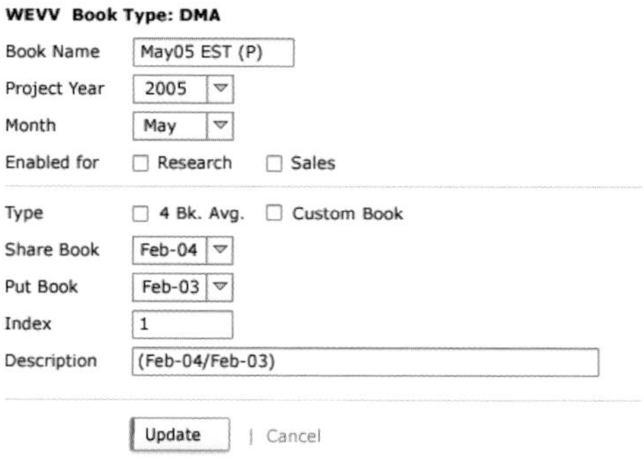

FIGURE 4.11
This advanced settings dialog
from AdConnections is an
example of where left-aligned
labels might make sense.

Labels Within Inputs

In cases where screen real estate is at a premium, combining labels and input fields into a single user interface element may be appropriate. Most commonly, this requires placing input labels inside their corresponding input fields (see Figure 4.12). Though it may be tempting to always halve the amount of screen space a form requires by using this method, there are a number of considerations worth calling out.

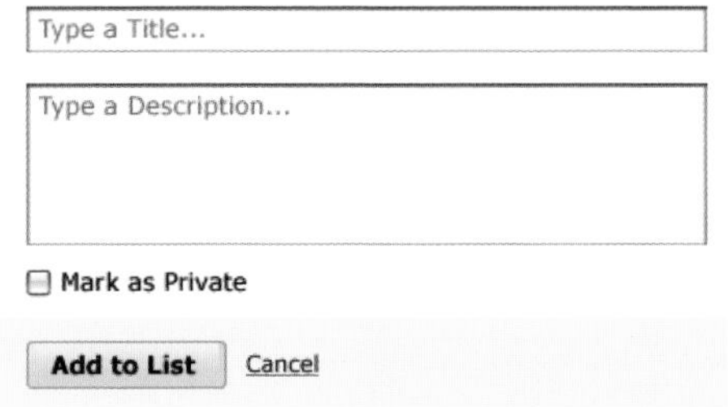

FIGURE 4.12
In this simple form, labels within input fields are displayed as gray text and include an ellipsis to distinguish them from data.

A reliable interaction for labels within forms requires the label to disappear quickly when users place their cursor into the input field so they can easily provide their answer. Early attempts at this interaction suffered from poor implementation. Sometimes, the label would disappear quickly. Other times, it would stay and become part of someone's answer. Even though we've made a lot of progress with dynamic Web technologies, making very sure your labels aren't sticking around in input fields when they shouldn't be is critical to making labels within input fields work.

Because labels within fields need to go away when people are entering their answer into an input field, the context for the answer is gone. So if you suddenly forget what question you're answering, tough luck—the label is nowhere to be found. As such, labels within inputs aren't a good solution for long or even medium-length forms. When you're done filling in the form, all the labels are gone! That makes it a bit hard to go back and check your answers. Single-question forms (like a search box), forms with just a couple inputs, or forms asking for very familiar data (like an address book) are much better candidates.

It's also generally a good rule not to use labels within inputs for non-obvious questions. That is, questions that may require people to reference the label while answering.

Lastly, labels within input fields should be presented in a way that makes it obvious at first glance that they are labels and not data. Perhaps the most common example seen in Figure 4.13 is the use of selection labels in drop-down menus. Here, a dash before and after the words "Select Month" is used to distinguish this label from an actual answer like "April" or "March."

FIGURE 4.13
Always ensure there is an obvious difference between labels and data. In this example, a set of dashes around a drop-down menu label distinguishes it from an actual answer.

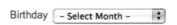

Mixed Alignments

I've often been asked if mixing label placement within a form or an application is problematic. After all, there may be cases within a form or an application where you want people to slow down and consider their options, in which case, left-aligned form fields might work best. In other cases, getting people through familiar inputs might steer you toward using right-aligned labels.

I actually haven't seen any conclusive data that mixing label placements within an application doesn't cause problems; rather, in my experience, context often wins out over consistency. But be sure to tread carefully when using different form layouts in the same application. While people might not be able to remember the differences between forms, they may subconsciously consider applications with many different kinds of forms "hard to use." Unless you have a very good reason to change alignments between different forms in the same application, a single layout will mitigate any consistency issues.

Changing label alignments within the same form, however, should really be avoided since it can cloud the clear path to completion people seek.

Best Practices

- Web form labels should use succinct, natural language and consistent capitalization to make answering the questions they pose as easy as possible.

- When you are trying to reduce completion times or if you need flexible label lengths for localization, consider top-aligned labels.

- When you have similar goals but vertical screen real estate constraints, consider right-aligned labels.

- When your form requires people to scan labels to learn what's required or to answer a few specific questions out of many, consider left-aligned labels.

- When you are under extreme space constraints for very short forms, labels within inputs may be a good solution. Just ensure that you have the right interactions and context in place.

- Make sure that you distinguish clearly between labels and data, especially when using labels within input fields.

- When considering different label alignments for different forms in a single application, think through the context versus consistency trade-off.

- Different label alignments in a single form will disrupt a clear path to completion and may confuse people.

Input Fields

O nce it's clear what questions should be on a form and how they should be presented, we need to provide people with a way to answer them. For this, we turn to input fields: checkboxes, radio buttons, drop-down menus, and text boxes of varying size.

Types of Input Fields

Because selecting which input field is right for a specific interaction is a fundamental interaction design problem, it's a bit outside the scope of this book.[1] However, a quick overview of when to use checkboxes, radio buttons, drop-down menus, and text boxes within Web forms is probably in order (see Figure 5.1 and Table 5.1).

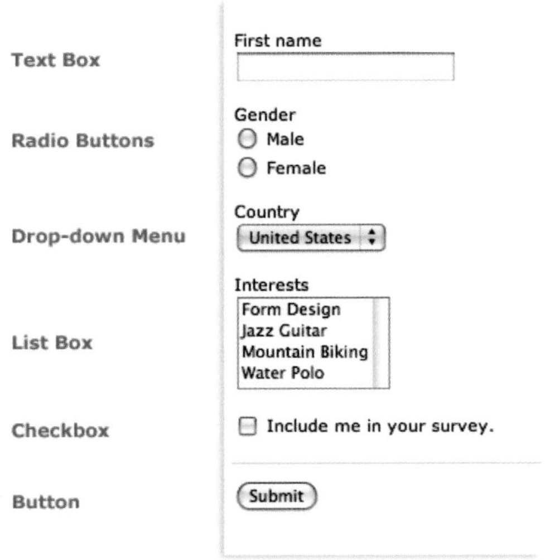

Text Box	First name
Radio Buttons	Gender ○ Male ○ Female
Drop-down Menu	Country United States
List Box	Interests Form Design Jazz Guitar Mountain Biking Water Polo
Checkbox	☐ Include me in your survey.
Button	Submit

FIGURE 5.1
The various types of input
fields found in Web forms.

---

[1]   For an in-depth discussion of when to use input fields, check out Bob Baxley's book: *Making the Web Work*, 2002, New Riders.

TABLE 5.1: TYPES OF INPUT FIELDS

INPUT FIELD	DESCRIPTION
Text boxes	Allow people to enter any number of characters (letters, numerals, or symbols) of their choosing. Text boxes can be single or multiple lines.
Radio buttons	Allow people to select exactly one choice from two or more always visible and mutually exclusive options. Because radio buttons are mutually exclusive, they should have a default value selected (more on this later). It's also a good idea to make sure both the radio button and its label can be selected to activate a radio button selection.
Checkboxes	Allow people to select any number of choices from a list of one or more options. Selecting one choice from one option is usually a yes or no question. As with radio buttons, it is a good idea for both the label and input field of checkboxes to be active.
Drop-down menus	Allow people to select exactly one choice from two or more mutually exclusive options. When not in use, drop-down menus only display the currently selected choice. As a result, they are better candidates than radio buttons for long lists of mutually exclusive choices since they use a minimum of screen real estate. Despite this advantage, it's generally a good idea to avoid really long lists in drop-down menus, especially when people are likely to be familiar with the options (like selecting the state they live in).
List boxes	List boxes can act as a set of radio buttons (allowing people to select exactly one choice from a set of mutually exclusive options) or as a set of checkboxes (allowing people to select any number of choices from a list of options). List boxes can be configured to show more options, like a drop-down menu, while still taking up less screen real estate than a list of radio buttons or checkboxes. Despite these advantages, the dual nature of list boxes (mutually exclusive single selection or multiple selection) tends to cause problems for many people. As a result, list boxes are rarely used in Web forms.

Note that I haven't included buttons in this list. There's a whole chapter devoted to them coming up!

Perspective: Bob Baxley
Author: Making the Web Work: Designing Effective Web Applications

Selecting Form Elements

One of the most challenging aspects of designing great forms is determining the most appropriate input controls. Because there is always more than one way to express a particular interaction or request a particular type of data, the form designer is invariably presented with a multiplicity of options that dramatically affect the user's experience.

In order to evaluate the range of design solutions, the design team needs to fully grasp the relative advantages and unique characteristics of each possibility. It is typical for the design team to struggle with trade-offs that pit click-efficiency against error prevention, learn-ability against efficiency, majority case against corner case, and flexibility against clarity. How these trade-offs are balanced ultimately depends on the judgment of the design team, optimizing for the specific audience and usage models involved.

The specification of quantity and type is a common issue for sites that sell tickets, and it provides a useful example of this design challenge. To begin, we should establish a few parameters about the audience and usage: (1) there are only three different types of tickets—General, Child, and Senior; (2) the vast majority of transactions involve small groups, typically fewer than six individuals; and (3) with few exceptions, visitors will buy tickets from the site less than once a month.

These parameters can be neatly summarized with this problem statement: a form that allows novice users to select up to six total tickets from any of three different classes. Because of the infrequency of use, the overall audience should be considered recurring novices, meaning that the design should optimize for learn-ability, obviousness, and error prevention.

There are three basic solutions to this problem, each relying on a different type of input control: text boxes, pull-down menus, and radio buttons.

The designers of Fandango.com opted for a solution that uses basic text boxes, an approach that is obvious and intuitive but that also presents some unexpected issues.

TICKET QUANTITY

General:	0	x $10.00 =	$0.00
Senior:	0	x $7.00 =	$0.00
Child:	0	x $7.00 =	$0.00

One issue with this solution, since many users don't realize they can use the Tab key to advance from one field to another, is how it leads users to skip back and forth between their mouse and keyboard. As a result, a significant number of visitors will have to bounce back and forth between their mouse and keyboard in order to complete the interaction.

A less obvious but more onerous issue is the solution's failure to prevent input errors. If the user types in a letter or noninteger value, the site pops open a JavaScript error alert—an unfortunate and unnecessary intrusion of the operating system.

Although the text box solution has some clear advantages in terms of obviousness and clarity, it has some equally clear disadvantages in terms of efficiency and error prevention.

Select Tickets					*per ticket
Ticket Type	Ticket Quantity	Service* Charge	Ticket* Price	Total*	
ADULT	0 ▾	$1.00	$10.25	$0.00 USD	
CHILD	0 ▾	$1.00	$7.25	$0.00 USD	
SENIOR	0 ▾	$1.00	$8.25	$0.00 USD	
Total	0	$0.00	$0.00	$0.00 USD	

Perspective: Bob Baxley (Continued)

An alternative solution seen at MovieTickets.com relies on drop-down menus. Again, it's an obvious solution but not without issues.

Although this solution provides a more aggressive stance against errors, preventing them before they can even occur, it does so by invoking a drop-down menu, the most complex and difficult input control available. While it's clearly a useful mechanism for controlling layout and visual presentation, unfortunately drop-down menus are hard to use, commonly overlooked, and often ignored.

As with the text box approach, the advantage of this solution at preventing errors comes at the cost of usability and obviousness.

Select Tickets								*per ticket
Ticket Type	Ticket Quantity					Ticket* Price	Service* Charge	Total
ADULT	● 0	○ 1	○ 2	○ 3	○ 4	$10.25	$1.00	$0.00 USD
CHILD	● 0	○ 1	○ 2	○ 3	○ 4	$7.25	$1.00	$0.00 USD
SENIOR	● 0	○ 1	○ 2	○ 3	○ 4	$8.25	$1.00	$0.00 USD
Total						$0.00	$0.00	$0.00 USD

A third solution utilizes radio buttons to collect the user's desired ticket quantity. Possessing the obviousness of the text box solution, it also has the error prevention advantages of the menu solution.

Unfortunately, it also requires considerably more input controls, 12 if the quantity is limited to four tickets from each class. Although the radio buttons can be presented in a simple graphic style, the sheer weight of 12 discreet interface elements is a bit overwhelming.

This basic analysis demonstrates that even seemingly simple data collection problems can be solved in multiple ways, with each solution presenting a unique combination of advantages and disadvantages. The job of the designer is to fully explore and analyze these possibilities in order to arrive at a solution that best satisfies the unique needs of the audience and application.

Field Lengths

Because input fields provide people with a way to answer the questions we ask, they also provide us with an opportunity to help people with their answers. The way we display input fields can produce valuable clues on how they should be filled in. Human Factors professionals call these clues *affordances.*[2]

For example, a handle on a door that looks like it should be pulled provides a valuable affordance. By virtue of its appearance, it lets people know how they can open the door: by pulling instead of pushing. Input fields can work in a similar way.

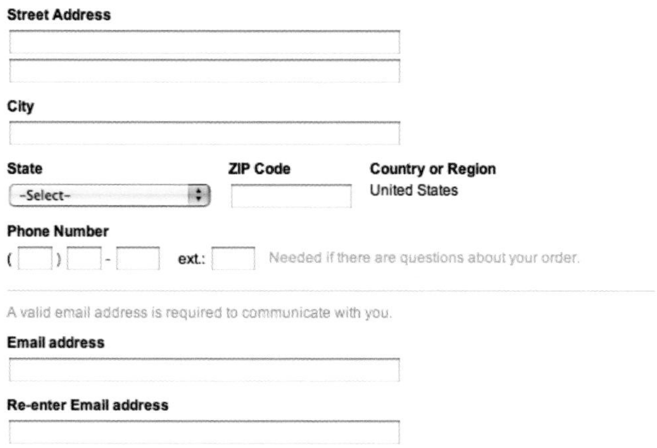

Street Address

City

State — –Select–   **ZIP Code**   **Country or Region** United States

Phone Number

( ) - ext: Needed if there are questions about your order.

A valid email address is required to communicate with you.

Email address

Re-enter Email address

FIGURE 5.2

The different text box lengths on this eBay Express form provide an affordance that helps people understand how to answer questions.

In the eBay Express example shown in Figure 5.2, the size of the zip code input matches the size of an actual zip code in the United States: 5 digits. The size of the phone number text boxes match the number of digits in a standard phone number in the United States. The rest of the text boxes are a consistent length that provides enough room for a complete answer.

---

[2]   For further information about affordances, check out Donald Norman's book, *The Design of Everyday Things,* 2002 Basic Books

Contrast eBay's approach with the Billing Information form from Macy's in Figure 5.3. In this example, all the text boxes are displayed with a uniform length, regardless of the type of answer people should provide. In other words, there are no affordances provided to help people give good answers. Instead, Macy's had to resort to help text that stipulated the number of digits their zip code input field required (xxxxx 5 digits only). This text could have been avoided by simply making the input field the right size.

FIGURE 5.3
Macy's opted for a consistent input length for primarily aesthetic reasons. However, this approach doesn't capitalize on natural affordances that can help people provide answers.

Because affordances provide valuable clues about how to structure answers, people will naturally consider those clues when they are thinking about how to fill in an input field. If that input field is arbitrarily sized, you may leave people thinking about what that means for no reason. For example, on the form from Tick in Figure 5.4, almost every input is a different size. That may leave people wondering "Should my Web address be much shorter than my company name?" or "Why such a long input for my email—am I missing something?"

Said another way, if this input field is long but my answer is short, have I misunderstood the question? Best not to make people think too much and instead use a consistent length for all the fields that don't benefit from clear affordances.

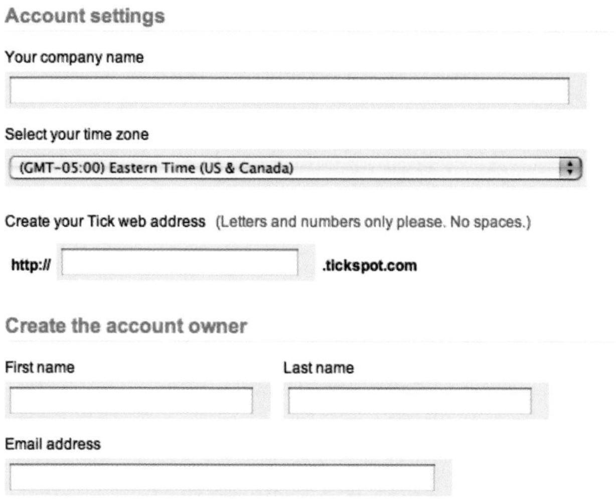

Account settings

Your company name

Select your time zone

(GMT–05:00) Eastern Time (US & Canada)

Create your Tick web address (Letters and numbers only please. No spaces.)

http://   .tickspot.com

Create the account owner

First name   Last name

Email address

FIGURE 5.4
Varying input sizes
abound on this form
from Tick.

Required Fields

I'm going to interrupt this chapter for a quick pop quiz: What does an asterisk next to an input field mean?

Many people will answer "It means this input is required so I have to provide an answer." Many—but not all. As is common with all Web conventions (de facto standards that have organically emerged online), there are exceptions to this rule. In fact, some Web sites use an asterisk to indicate optional input fields (Figure 5.5) instead of required ones.

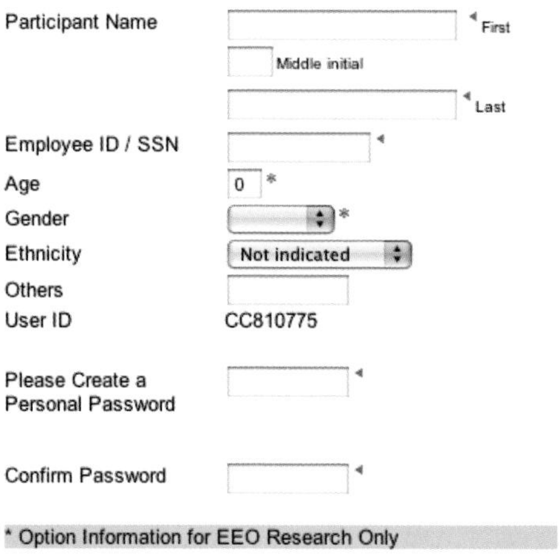

Participant Name ◄ First
Middle initial
◄ Last
Employee ID / SSN ◄
Age   0   *
Gender   *
Ethnicity   Not indicated
Others
User ID   CC810775

Please Create a ◄
Personal Password

Confirm Password ◄

* Option Information for EEO Research Only

FIGURE 5.5
Asterisks on the Hogan sign-up
form indicate optional fields!
Not what most people would
expect.

In both cases, the more important question is when to indicate required or optional input fields at all (see Figure 5.6). When discussing content organization earlier, I made the point that any question that doesn't need an answer should get dropped to make it easier for people to complete the form. So you might argue that there should never be a situation where we need to distinguish between required and optional inputs, right?

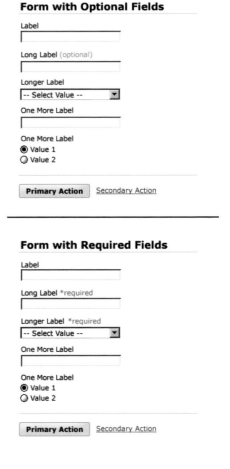

FIGURE 5.6
Indicating optional or required fields next to input field labels.

Well, unfortunately the complexity of information many forms need to collect doesn't make it that easy on us. Many times there actually are good reasons for indicating what is required when updating or creating a record online. In particular, when a Web form has lots of input fields but only a few of them are required, indicating what *has* to be answered can be quite useful. It helps to think of required input fields as decisions people have to make. If they don't and try to complete the form, they'll get an error!

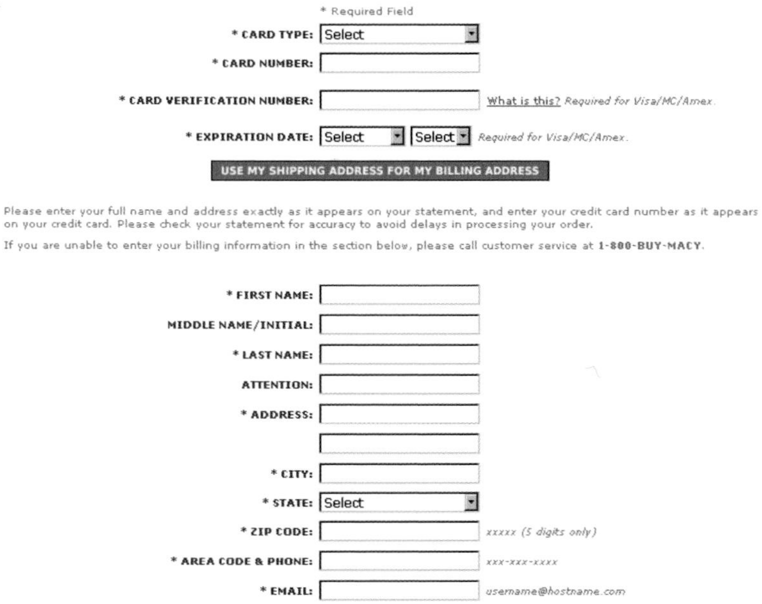

* Required Field

* CARD TYPE: Select

* CARD NUMBER:

* CARD VERIFICATION NUMBER: _What is this? Required for Visa/MC/Amex._

* EXPIRATION DATE: Select Select _Required for Visa/MC/Amex._

USE MY SHIPPING ADDRESS FOR MY BILLING ADDRESS

Please enter your full name and address exactly as it appears on your statement, and enter your credit card number as it appears on your credit card. Please check your statement for accuracy to avoid delays in processing your order.

If you are unable to enter your billing information in the section below, please call customer service at 1-800-BUY-MACY.

* FIRST NAME:

MIDDLE NAME/INITIAL:

* LAST NAME:

ATTENTION:

* ADDRESS:

* CITY:

* STATE: Select

* ZIP CODE: _xxxxx (5 digits only)_

* AREA CODE & PHONE: _xxx-xxx-xxxx_

* EMAIL: _username@hostname.com_

FIGURE 5.7

On Macy's every input is required and marked as such except for Middle Name and Attention. It may be clearer to simply mark these two fields as optional instead.

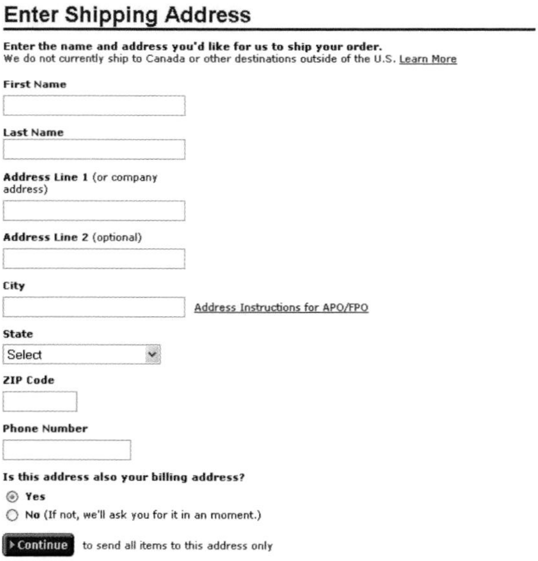

Enter Shipping Address

Enter the name and address you'd like for us to ship your order.
We do not currently ship to Canada or other destinations outside of the U.S. Learn More

First Name

Last Name

Address Line 1 (or company address)

Address Line 2 (optional)

City
Address Instructions for APO/FPO

State
Select

ZIP Code

Phone Number

Is this address also your billing address?
⦿ Yes
◯ No (If not, we'll ask you for it in an moment.)

▶ Continue to send all items to this address only

FIGURE 5.8

On Wal-Mart, every input is required but one (Address Line 2). Instead of marking everything required, the one optional field has been clearly marked optional, thereby reducing the amount of information on the form.

Conversely, indicating which input fields are optional is useful when most questions require an answer but a few do not. Neither indicator is particularly useful when the input fields are either all required or all optional. In these circumstances, indicating required or optional fields adds unnecessary information to the form that people then have to pause and consider.

Similarly, indicating the majority case (most input fields are required or optional) versus the minority case (just a few input fields are required or optional) increases the amount of information that overlies a form. This difference can be seen by comparing the Macy's and Wal-Mart examples in this section (Figures 5.7 and 5.8). Macy's uses a lot of visual information to tell you the two fields are optional. Wal-Mart uses one word to tell you a single field is optional.

The Wal-Mart example also highlights why it's better to be explicit when indicating what is optional or required. Literally including the phrase "optional" after a label is much clearer than any visual symbol you could use to mean the same thing. Someone may always wonder "what does this asterisk mean?" and have to go hunting for a legend that explains things (see Figure 5.9). Of course, there needs to be a legend to find! On Barnes & Noble's site shown in Figure 5.10, no legend exists that explains the use of an asterisk.

Some people will argue that a site's Web forms should be consistent throughout, and therefore every required input field should be indicated as such, regardless of whether or not there are any optional input fields on the form. While this may be useful in forms that require several pages to complete, the variety of Web forms people encounter online makes it hard to imagine that they will remember a specific site's system of indicating required input fields across the one to two forms they encounter.

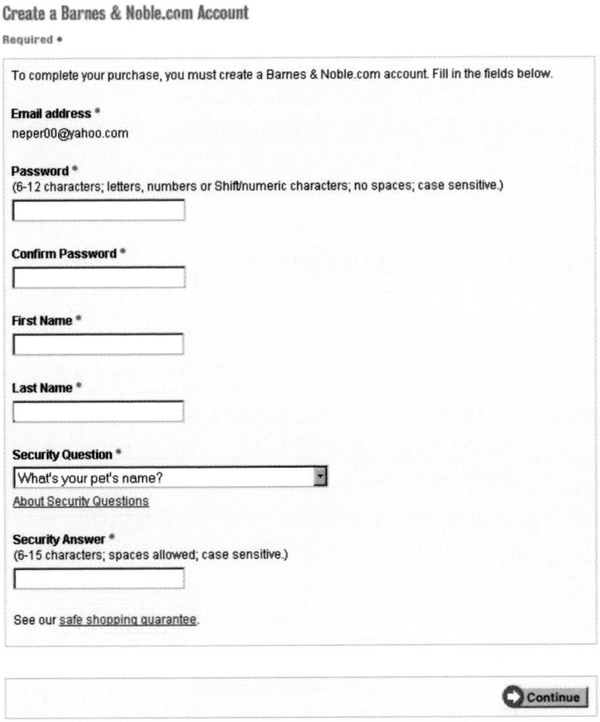

Create a Barnes & Noble.com Account

Required *

To complete your purchase, you must create a Barnes & Noble.com account. Fill in the fields below.

Email address *
neper00@yahoo.com

Password *
(6-12 characters; letters, numbers or Shift/numeric characters; no spaces; case sensitive.)

Confirm Password *

First Name *

Last Name *

Security Question *
What's your pet's name?
About Security Questions

Security Answer *
(6-15 characters; spaces allowed; case sensitive.)

See our safe shopping guarantee.

Continue

FIGURE 5.9
On Barnes & Noble's Web site, all the input fields are required and marked as such —why?

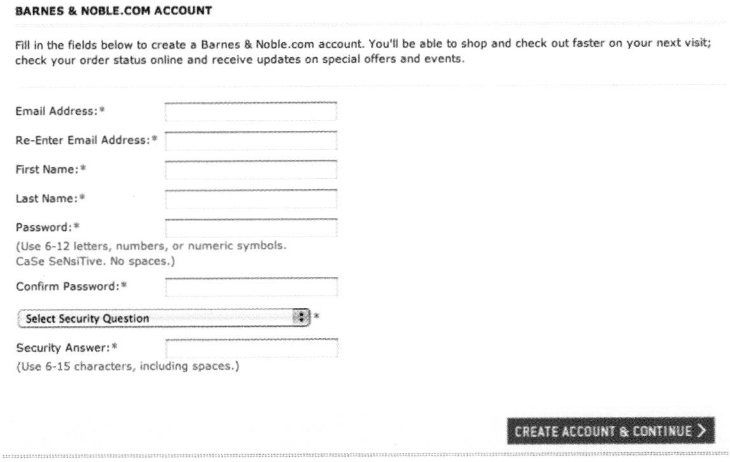

BARNES & NOBLE.COM ACCOUNT

Fill in the fields below to create a Barnes & Noble.com account. You'll be able to shop and check out faster on your next visit; check your order status online and receive updates on special offers and events.

Email Address: *

Re-Enter Email Address: *

First Name: *

Last Name: *

Password: *
(Use 6-12 letters, numbers, or numeric symbols. CaSe SeNsiTive. No spaces.)

Confirm Password: *

Select Security Question *

Security Answer: *
(Use 6-15 characters, including spaces.)

CREATE ACCOUNT & CONTINUE >

FIGURE 5.10
When Barnes & Noble redesigned its site, the company kept the asterisks that indicated every input field was required but removed the text that explained what the asterisk indicated.

If you do opt for a visual system to indicate required input fields, carefully consider where you place the indicators on the form. Indicators next to labels give people a way to scan a form quickly and determine what questions require an answer (Figure 5.11). Indicators aligned with input fields can make this difficult because of the variety of shapes and sizes that input fields can have (Figure 5.12).

基本情報 ＊は必須項目です

お名前（氏／名）＊	（全角）
フリガナ（氏／名）＊	（全角カタカナ）
Ｅメールアドレス＊	（半角数字）
Ｅメールアドレス（確認）＊	（半角数字）
携帯アドレス	選択してください （半角数字）
携帯アドレス（確認）	選択してください （半角数字）
郵便番号＊	〒 － （半角数字）住所表示 7桁の郵便番号を入力して「住所表示」ボタンを押して下さい。 県／市区町村名を郵便番号から自動検索し、入力されます。
都道府県＊	
市区町村＊	（全角）
それ以降の住所（丁目／番地など）＊	（全角）＊丁目／番地を必ずご入力ください
ビル／マンション名	（全角）
電話番号＊	－ － （半角数字）
メンバー登録＊	○ゲスト購入する ◉会員登録する

戻る　　　次へ進む

基本情報入力 ＊この内容は必須項目となります・すべての項目にご記入下さい。

お名前	様＊ （全角）
ふりがな	さま＊ （全角ひらがな）
ご住所 〒	－ ＊ 〒→住所 （半角数字） （郵便番号から住所が検索できます）
都道府県選択	
	市区町村＊ （全角）
	番地等＊ （全角／半角英数字）
	建物ビル名等 （全角／半角英数字）
電話番号	－ － ＊ （半角数字）
ＦＡＸ番号	－ － （半角数字）
メールアドレス	＊ （半角英数字）
メールアドレス（確認）	＊ （半角英数字）
パスワード	＊ （4文字以上8文字以下の半角英数字）
パスワード（確認）	＊ （4文字以上8文字以下の半角英数字）

FIGURES 5.11 & 5.12
Try to scan each of these forms to see what input fields are required. When indicators are aligned with input fields instead of labels, it's much harder to get a sense of which questions must be answered.

オプション情報入力 ＊以下の内容はご希望の方のみご回答下さい。また、初回登録時以外は表示されません。

性別 ○男性 ○女性 ◉設定しない＊
生年月日 1930 年 月 日＊
既婚／未婚 ○既婚 ○未婚＊
家族構成（人数） 人（本人含む）＊
どこでで±0を知りましたか？

☐広告　☐新聞／雑誌の記事（紙/誌名　　　）　☐友人／知人から
☐テレビ／ラジオ　☐インターネット上の情報（サイト名　　　）　☐検索エンジン
☐イベント／店頭　☐メールマガジン（誌名　　　）　☐その他

Perspective: Micah Alpern
Director of Social Search, Yahoo! Inc.

The Structural Design of Forms

Powerful design comes from the reuse of a small number of simple patterns. This is the essence of the power that a grid provides for visual designers. For example, grids with sweeping horizontal and vertical lines help designers place new elements on the page, while considering their relationship to the whole. Similarly, interaction designers have begun using consistent interaction patterns to simplify design decisions and provide global consistency.[3] So what patterns of structure underlie a form?

THE CORE OF A FORM IS AN INPUT

Inputs are atomic UI components designed to receive user feedback upon which all forms are built.

Here you see multiple inputs of different types, but with the same underlying structure.

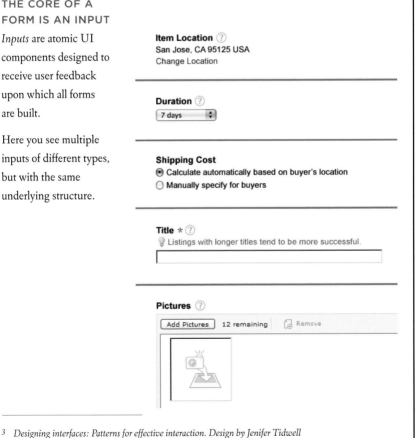

___

3 *Designing interfaces: Patterns for effective interaction. Design by Jenifer Tidwell*

Perspective: Micah Alpern (Continued)

Inputs can take many shapes, but the basic pattern is the same: title, data, actions. This basic pattern repeats again and again across multiple types of inputs and at multiple levels within a form (for example, at an input, a section, a dialog, or a page).

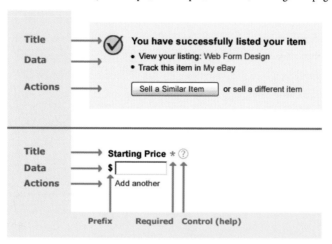

This structure helps define the visual design as expressed through style (fonts, weights, color, icons) and layout (alignment, margins, and padding,).

GROUPING INPUTS

A Group is two or more inputs with some kind of relationship. Three of the most frequent types of Group inputs are Compound inputs, Related inputs, and Parent/Child inputs. These input types are important because they are each suited to different types of problems, and they handle errors and dependencies differently.

Perspective: Micah Alpern (Continued)

Three different types of groups include the following:

STRUCTURAL DESIGN

The form examples here are taken from the pattern language we developed when redesigning the selling processes at eBay. By thinking about the design structurally, we forced ourselves to consider the following questions, for each new UI element:

- What kind of thing is this?

- How are other things of this kind treated?

- What is the relationship of this element to all other elements?

- Can we simplify the design by consolidating this kind of element with others or by extending the relationship between this element and others?

Compound Input

| Input | Input |

Scheduled Start ⑦

| Saturday, Feb 23 ⬍ | 8:30 AM ⬍ | PST

Related Inputs

| Input | | Input |

Number of Lots ⑦   **Items per Lot** ⑦

Parent/Child

| Input |
| Input |

Selling Format ⑦

Online Auction ⬍

Starting Price   **Quantity**

$ [   ]   [   ] items

Duration

7 days ⬍

By consistently and repeatedly asking these questions, we created a coherent design whose underlying structural patterns made the interface simple and concise.

Input Groups

For many of the questions we ask within Web forms, there's a common way to respond. Mailing addresses, for example, have a widely known structure that can be leveraged to help people understand how to answer questions about shipping or billing locations. Other examples include first name and last name, date and time, or the parts of a phone number.

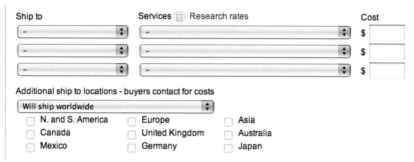

FIGURE 5.13

The grouping of inputs on eBay's Sell Your Item format represents a meaningful structure.

Input field groups can be used to reflect meaningful relationships between the different parts of an input. Consider the eBay shipping selection inputs shown in Figure 5.13. Multiple shipping services are available each with a structure of Ship to, using a Service, at a specific Cost. Similarly, the grouping of additional locations is governed by a global control: will ship worldwide or only to specific locations, which are listed below.

These input groups can be utilized within forms to provide additional clues on how questions should be answered.

Flexible Inputs

Though there's more than one right way to answer a question, many Web forms aren't that flexible. Because of technical, legal, or business constraints, there's often a specific way people need to answer a question for their response to be considered valid.

Take the seemingly simple question of "What's your phone number?" We can provide some simple help text next to the input (as you'll see in Chapter 7) to let people know how they should answer the question: "Use xxx-xxx-xxxx as the format for your answer." We can structure the input fields and their affordances to accept only a specific format: three text boxes of the appropriate length separated by the appropriate punctuation.

Or we can provide a flexible input field that allows people to answer the question the way they wish (see Figure 5.14). In our phone number example, there are basically five different ways a valid phone number could be specified. A simple script can check to see if one of these has been used and submit the information in whatever format the back-end system requires. The chore of adhering to a specific format is taken off the person providing an answer and instead given to a small bit of code.

FIGURE 5.14
Input fields can be made flexible enough to accept multiple formats of a valid answer.

Another example of flexible input fields comes from the invitation form on Renkoo, shown in Figure 5.15. When specifying a place to meet, this input field allows three kinds of answers. If people just want to type in a location, they can do so. If they'd also like to include an address or a map, a single click exposes the appropriate suboptions. If someone would like to include a map but doesn't know the address, he can search for a place and have the address filled in automatically for them. All three of these options result in valid answers. How much or how little information is provided is up to the person filling in the form.

FIGURE 5.15

A flexible input on the Renkoo invitation form.

In the interests of full disclosure, this example doesn't let people know they can search for a place up front. It's an option hidden behind a click. Nonetheless, I think it demonstrates how input fields could be considered complete and valid with varying amounts of information or different formats from people.

It's also important to note that despite allowing answers of varying detail, this interaction makes it easy to provide the simplest answer. If you just want to type in a place, nothing stands in your way. Flexibility at the expense of how easily people can provide the most common answer is likely to do more harm than good.

Best Practices

- Use the right input field for the type of question you are asking: Does it require a yes or no answer; a selection from mutually exclusive options; etc.?

- Where possible, ensure that field lengths provide meaningful affordances that help people answer questions effectively.

- Otherwise, utilize a consistent length that provides enough room for correct answers.

- Try to avoid optional input fields in forms.

- If most of the inputs on a form are required, indicate the few that are optional.

- If most of the inputs on a form are optional, indicate the few that are required.

- When indicating what form fields are either required or optional, text is the most clear. However, the * symbol is relatively well understood to mean required.

- If you do use * to indicate required fields, don't forget a legend that explains what it indicates.

- Associate required or optional indicators with input labels to give people an easy way to see which questions need to be answered.

- If there's a natural structure among input fields that provides a valuable clue on how to answer a question, look for ways to group these inputs visually to clearly communicate that structure.

- When there's clearly more than one way to format an answer correctly, consider using a flexible input field.

- Ensure that flexible inputs don't make providing easy answers more difficult.

CHAPTER 6

Actions

L abels provide the questions that forms ask people. Input fields give people a way to answer those questions. Neither of these items, however, actually lets people complete a form. That singular responsibility rests with actions.

Primary and Secondary Actions

A typical Web form usually enables several final actions (see Figure 6.1). Actions such as Submit, Save, or Continue are intended to enable completion, which is the primary goal of just about anyone who has started filling in a form. Because they enable the most important action on the form (completion), they can be referred to as *primary actions*.

FIGURE 6.1
Primary and secondary actions on a Web form can be represented in ways that illuminate their importance.

Secondary actions, on the other hand, tend to be less utilized and most often allow people to retract the data they've entered. Options like Cancel, Reset, or Go Back represent secondary actions that are counter to most people's primary goal of completing the form they began.

Because secondary actions can have negative consequences (see Figure 6.2), especially when used unintentionally, I've often argued they should be absent from forms. Imagine filling in a long form online only to hit the Reset button and have all your data erased.

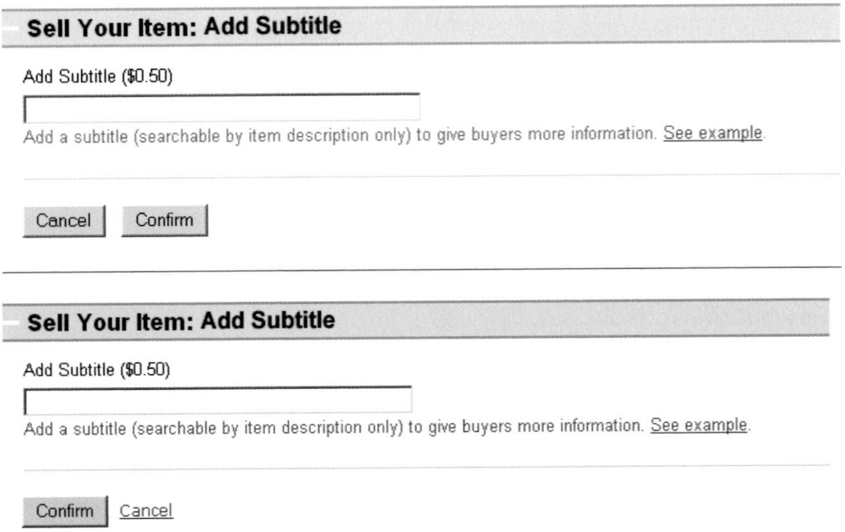

Sell Your Item: Add Subtitle

Add Subtitle ($0.50)

Add a subtitle (searchable by item description only) to give buyers more information. See example.

| Cancel | Confirm |

Sell Your Item: Add Subtitle

Add Subtitle ($0.50)

Add a subtitle (searchable by item description only) to give buyers more information. See example.

| Confirm | Cancel |

FIGURE 6.2
Even on very short forms like this one from eBay, secondary actions can be problematic. Which button would you have pressed? The redesign makes it much clearer.

That said, there are situations where secondary actions make sense (such as Save for Later, Preview, Export, etc.). Perhaps the most common example involves multiple page form wizards where people can move forward and backward through Web pages. Though it may be tempting to treat Previous and Next as equal actions in these circumstances, keeping people moving forward with a primary Continue action and a secondary Back action is likely to be more productive. After all, we want people to complete these forms, right?

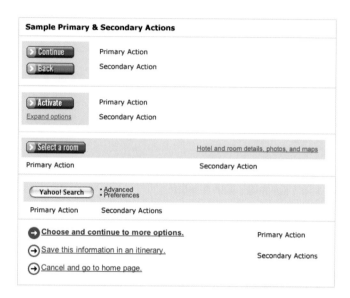

FIGURE 6.3
Various ways to distinguish primary and secondary actions include different button styles, combinations of buttons and links, and different links styles.

When you reduce the visual prominence of secondary actions, it minimizes the risk for potential errors and further directs people toward a successful outcome. But what's the best way to accomplish this distinction (see Figure 6.3)? How different should primary and secondary actions be and where should they be placed? To answer these questions, I ran a few tests with London-based usability firm Etre.[1]

In order to assess which presentation of primary and secondary actions might work best, we tested six variations on 23 people using eye-tracking and usability metrics. Participants were presented each of six designs in random order (to minimize familiarity biases) and asked to "Please complete the form fully and accurately." Though other options could have been tested, we selected these (Figure 6.4) based on a survey of the most commonly used solutions at the time we ran our test.

---

[1] The full results of the Etre study can be found at: http://www.lukew.com/resources/articles/PSactions.asp

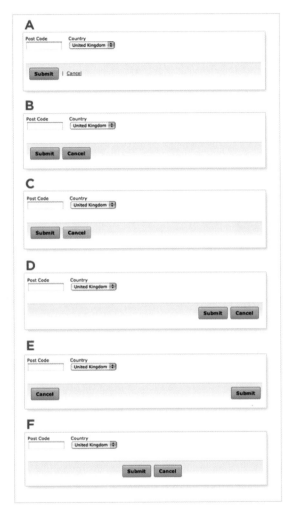

FIGURE 6.4
The set of primary and secondary action designs tested for this book.

People accomplished their task perfectly when using five of the six designs. Options A, B, C, D, and F achieved success rates of 100 percent, without causing people to make a single error. They also saw comparable task completion times and received high satisfaction ratings. Option E, as we'll see later, didn't fare as well.

Of the options we tested, option B performed best of all. Fixations were shorter and fewer in number when using this design (see Figure 6.5). And people were also able to complete the task more quickly and efficiently than they did when using the others. In fact, option B required an average of 2.1 seconds less to complete than the options that visually distinguished primary and secondary actions.

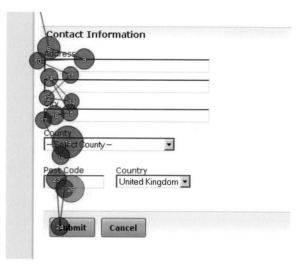

FIGURE 6.5
Eye fixations from a single participant when both primary and secondary actions were visually identical. Image provided by Etre.

But when using option B, a number of people expressed concern that they "could quite easily click the wrong button." Several people also spoke positively about the designs that made "Cancel" stand out in some way (options A and C in Figure 6.4), mentioning that the visual distinction helped them avoid taking the wrong action (see Figure 6.6). Both options A and C also had a higher satisfaction rating than option B.

This combination of positive qualitative data and small quantitative differences in performance is the reason I continue to recommend visually distinguishing secondary actions when they can't be removed from a form.

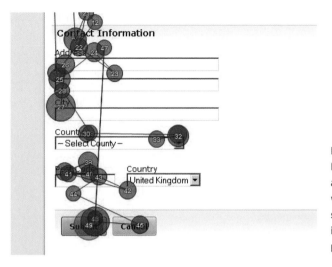

FIGURE 6.6
Eye fixations from a single participant when primary and secondary differed in color. Image provided by Etre.

Several people have suggested to me that a proven way to clearly distinguish between primary and secondary actions is through the use of green for the primary action and red for the secondary action (see Figure 6.7). Displaying either the button itself or an icon within it in these colors makes a clear distinction between successful (green) actions and unsuccessful (red) actions. Personally, I'm always hesitant to use red to label any action, due to that color's close association with errors. Red is used so often to indicate something bad has happened on a form—as we'll see later in the book—that I'm quite wary of using it to represent either secondary or primary actions.

FIGURE 6.7
Color and shape distinctions like those on Wufoo.com can be used to distinguish primary and secondary actions, but red text should be reserved for errors.

One way to ensure that secondary actions do not result in catastrophic losses of data is to provide an automatic Undo behavior. Rather than asking people to confirm that they'd like to reset a form when they click Reset, simply replace the Reset button with an Undo button after they select it.

Of course, this requires your form to store people's data as they enter it, but that's a small price to pay for preventing catastrophic data loss.

Placement

In the tests I ran with Etre, only Option E performed quite poorly. We found that 26 percent of the people tested mistakenly clicked the Cancel button when attempting the task with this design, while many more lingered over it before realizing that they were about to make a mistake (see Figure 6.8).

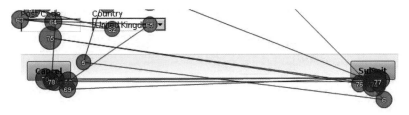

FIGURE 6.8
Eye fixations from a single participant when primary and secondary were separated. Image provided by Etre.

People's fixations were longest when using Option F. And, as a whole, they were around six seconds slower when using Option F than they were when using Option B, which is a considerable gap when you consider that the placement of the buttons was the only thing that differed between the two.

We believe that this was because they expected the two buttons to be left-aligned (i.e., to appear directly below the last input field on the page) and upon finding that this wasn't the case, they had to search around to find them (see Figure 6.9).

FIGURE 6.9
Eye fixations from a single participant when primary and secondary actions were centered on the bottom of a form. Image provided by Etre.

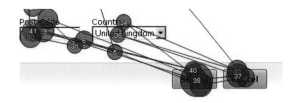

According to the data we collected, the most effective designs of the six we tested all shared a common characteristic: they presented their Submit and Cancel options left-aligned with the input fields and labels above them.

These findings map well to our first form design principle: illuminate a clear path to completion. You should be conscious of where you place form actions, since primary actions directly aligned with input fields tend to decrease completion times and, as we know, the less time people have to spend on your forms, the happier they will be.

Actions in Progress

Let's assume that you've answered all the questions on a form correctly and selected the primary action to signify you're done. Then what? If nothing changes, perhaps the site didn't register your click. Is your information being processed? When in doubt, most people will try again. Depending on how a form is developed, this may lead to a duplicate submission. Now you've done what you were trying to accomplish twice!

One potential solution is to include a warning that asks people not to click on a primary action twice, as seen in Figure 6.10. But this unfairly places the burden on the person who is filling in the form. It's an "inside out" solution.

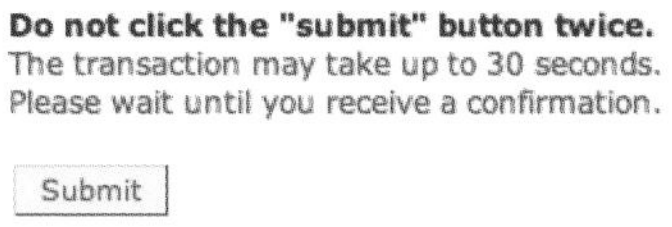

Do not click the "submit" button twice.
The transaction may take up to 30 seconds.
Please wait until you receive a confirmation.

[Submit]

FIGURE 6.10
Avoid excessive instructions that tell people not to press Submit more than once.

A better answer is to replace the active primary action with an animation or text message that lets people know their submission was accepted and is in progress (see Figure 6.11).

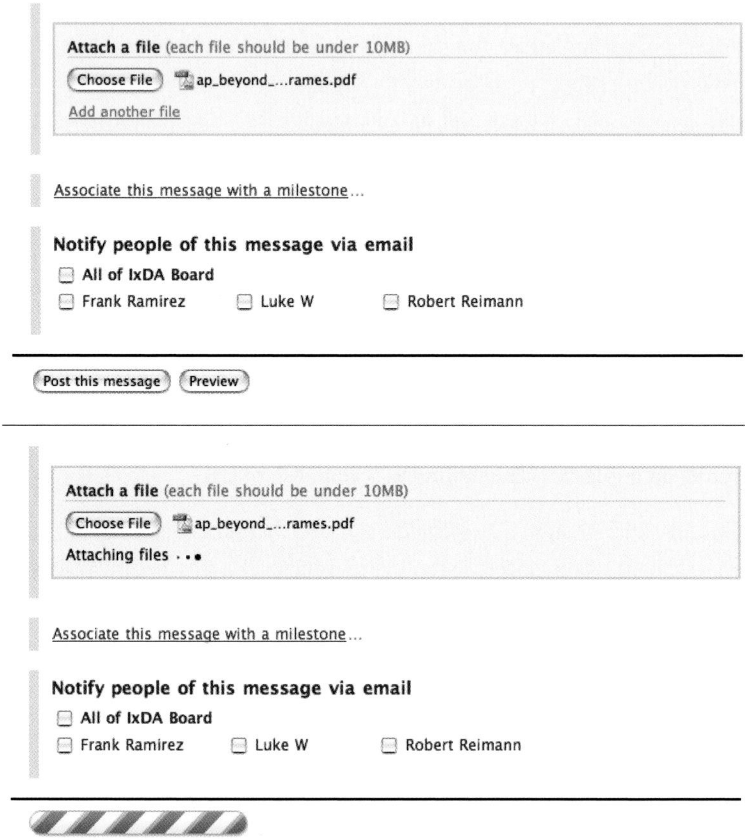

Attach a file (each file should be under 10MB)

(Choose File) ap_beyond_...rames.pdf

Add another file

Associate this message with a milestone...

Notify people of this message via email

☐ All of IxDA Board

☐ Frank Ramirez   ☐ Luke W   ☐ Robert Reimann

(Post this message) (Preview)

Attach a file (each file should be under 10MB)

(Choose File) ap_beyond_...rames.pdf

Attaching files · ·●

Associate this message with a milestone...

Notify people of this message via email

☐ All of IxDA Board

☐ Frank Ramirez   ☐ Luke W   ☐ Robert Reimann

FIGURE 6.11

Basecamp provides progress indicators for form submission and file uploads using animated images.

Any additional process that will need some time to complete can be communicated in the same way. In the form from the Basecamp project management application shown in Figure 6.11, not only is the primary action button replaced with a progress indicator animation, but an animated image and text indicates that a file is being uploaded as well. In all likelihood, that's what is causing the delay in submitting the form. The combination of both progress indicators makes it clear.

Forms with clearly defined answers could even elect to disable the primary action until all the questions within the form have been answered with valid information. This approach requires a dynamic system that "knows" what constitutes a valid reply for every question on the form and when all the questions have been answered (see Figure 6.12). Only then is the primary action made active.

FIGURE 6.12
Basecamp's sign-up form disables the Submit button until all inputs have valid answers.

Unless every question on a form must be answered, determining when people are done—and thereby activating the primary action—can be problematic. Therefore, this method should be avoided on forms that include any optional questions.

It's also worth noting that despite being disabled, the primary action in Figure 6.12 is always visible. This provides a clear path to completion because people can always see the action that will allow them to complete the form. Contrast this approach with the example in Figure 6.13, which only shows the primary action when the form is completed. This may leave people scratching their heads as they try to determine how to complete the form.

Welcome to Marriott's Wired for Business package! With the power of High Speed Internet Access and the convenience of Unlimited Local and Domestic Long Distance calling, you are now empowered to work at the speed of office.

Benefit from a more productive work environment that allows you to navigate the web up to 50 times faster than dial-up and the ability to simultaneously dial and receive calls while working online.

○ If you want to activate Wired for Business
WIRED-FOR-BUSINESS Package; $ 9.95 noon to noon per day of your stay (If you wish to purchase Wired for Business for a single day only, contact the front desk.)
• Unlimited iBAHN High-Speed Internet Access

• Unlimited local and long-distance phone calls (within US)

• Guest room Internet and Public Space Wireless roaming included in this package

FIGURE 6.13

The ibahn activation form doesn't display a primary action until someone selects the radio button. Not only does this form obscure a path to completion by hiding the primary action, but it also incorrectly uses radio buttons, which should never appear alone (see Chapter 5).

Welcome to Marriott's Wired for Business package! With the power of High Speed Internet Access and the convenience of Unlimited Local and Domestic Long Distance calling, you are now empowered to work at the speed of office.

Benefit from a more productive work environment that allows you to navigate the web up to 50 times faster than dial-up and the ability to simultaneously dial and receive calls while working online.

⦿ If you want to activate Wired for Business
WIRED-FOR-BUSINESS Package; $ 9.95 noon to noon per day of your stay (If you wish to purchase Wired for Business for a single day only, contact the front desk.)
• Unlimited iBAHN High-Speed Internet Access

• Unlimited local and long-distance phone calls (within US)

• Guest room Internet and Public Space Wireless roaming included in this package

>> Activate

Agree and Submit

Many registration forms require people not only to answer a series of questions about themselves (name, email, password, etc.), but also to agree to a set of conditions governing their pending membership. Most of these forms have a legal requirement to ensure that new members explicitly agree to these "terms of service."

A common approach to solving this issue is separating the agreement and the primary action of submitting the form into two separate elements: a checkbox for agreement and a button for completion. One potential problem with this technique is that people may skip over the terms of service checkbox, assuming it is an opt-in for marketing materials, newsletters, or spam. Then when they try to complete the form, they will receive an error telling them they must agree to the site's terms of service. This process may cause frustration or, even worse, abandonment.

It doesn't help that in many situations, the marketing opt-ins are listed right next to the terms of service agreement (see Figure 6.14). "Send me marketing materials" is often default checked, and most people want to uncheck it. Terms of Service, directly below, is the exact opposite. It is default unchecked, and most people want to check it so they can complete the form.

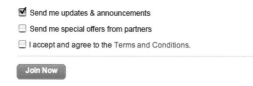

FIGURE 6.14

Common options for marketing materials and terms of service agreements.

Luckily, there are opportunities to provide a cleaner path to completion. Instead of a separate question to address the terms of service, the primary action can cover both the terms of service agreement and form completion (see Figures 6.15 and 6.16).

FIGURES 6.15 & 6.16

Two approaches for combining terms of service agreement and form completion into a single action.

Depending on the legal requirements of a site, the terms of service can be governed by a primary call to action that explicitly includes a legal agreement, for example, a button labeled "I agree and move forward" or one that infers it through text preceding the primary action "by clicking register below, I agree."

The advantage of both these options is that they require one less explicit question for people to answer. However, the second option has the added advantage of not complicating the primary call to action. Consider the difference between "Buy Now" and "Agree & Buy Now." One is clearly more directly aligned with people's goals of buying a product than the other.

Best Practices

- Avoid secondary actions on forms whenever possible. Provide people with a single path to completion.

- If secondary actions are required, ensure that there is a clear visual distinction between the primary and secondary actions.

- When you are distributing the questions in a form across multiple Web pages, primary actions move people closer to completion and secondary actions allow them to go back.

- Align primary actions with input fields to create a clear path to completion.

- If you do choose to include potentially destructive secondary actions like Reset or Clear in your form, provide people with an easy way to undo them.

- Clearly communicate when a form is being processed to avoid duplicate submissions.

- Don't rely on help text urging people not to hit a primary action twice; instead, disable the primary action button and prevent them from doing so.

- Consider opportunities to streamline legal requirements by combining terms of service agreements with primary actions.

CHAPTER 7

Help Text

Although the way we phrase labels and display input fields can provide useful clues on how to provide answers, these elements alone are sometimes not enough. In these cases, it's common practice to resort to "telling" people how they should answer a question by including help text next to a form's labels or input fields.

Help text is basically just a set of messages that help people complete forms successfully. This means that help messages are structurally similar to the error and success messages we'll look at in Chapter 8 and, as a result, share many best practices.

When to Help

Tempting as it may be simply to spell out how people should fill in an input field, help text isn't the holy grail of Web form completion. For starters, if excessive instructions are required to explain how to complete your form, then chances are the questions you are asking are either phrased poorly, too complex, or just plain unnecessary. Excessive help text may be an indicator that it's time to go back to the drawing board and make sure the questions you are asking people are the right ones (see Figure 7.1).

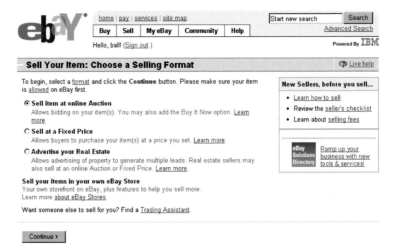

FIGURE 7.1
On this eBay form, excessive help text makes a single choice seem overly complex. There are over 10 different ways to get help picking one of three radio buttons.

Help text can also be problematic because people tend not to read instructions presented onscreen. Relying on a set of instructions to explain your form will lead to trouble when those instructions are bypassed by most people (see Figure 7.2). In fact, eye-tracking research shows that many people jump directly to the first input field when presented with a form. It seems to be a natural tendency to want to start filling things in. We just want to get this form done and move on!

Yet there are cases when instructional text is appropriate. In particular, concise bits of help text are most useful in the following circumstances:

- When forms ask for unfamiliar data: What's a PAC code?

- When people question why they are being asked for specific data: Why do you need to know my date of birth?

- When people may be concerned about the security or privacy of their data: Is my credit card number safe here?

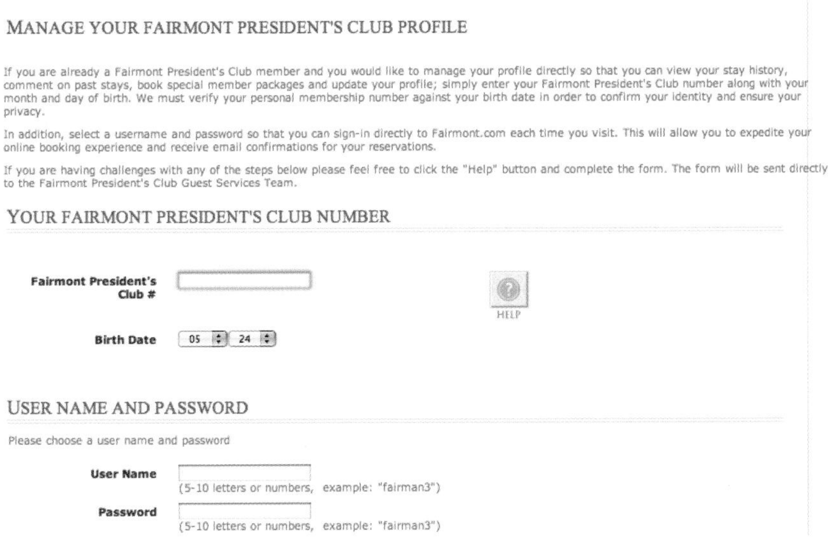

FIGURE 7.2
The three paragraphs of instructional text on this Fairmont Hotels page are likely to get passed over by most people.

- When there are recommended ways of providing data: Separate your tags with commas, please.

- When certain data fields are optional or required when the bulk of the form is not.

In these cases, a clear and concise bit of help text adjacent to an input field tends to do the trick. In the videoegg sign-up form in Figure 7.3, the site recommends that your password be four characters or more and tells you that if you are concerned about providing your email address, don't worry —it doesn't spam. Period. In both cases, the minimum amount of help text needed to get the message across was used. If only all our forms were so simple.

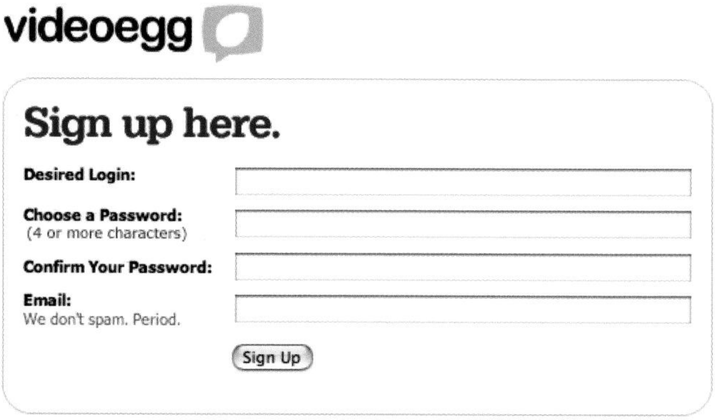

FIGURE 7.3
On videoegg's
sign-up form, the
minimum amount
of help text
required is used
to help people
answer questions.

In reality, there are many forms that require people to provide lots of obscure data in obscure formats, as well as forms where people are likely to question what they are being asked and why. In some of these cases, the amount of help text necessary for each input field could quickly overwhelm a form, making it appear intimidating or complex. For these forms, it may make sense to consider using a dynamic help system.

Dynamic help systems can be automatically triggered or accessed through explicit user action. Automatic triggered systems reveal applicable help text when people naturally engage with a form. Actions like moving between input fields or groups of input fields result in the display of useful help text.

User-activated help systems, on the other hand, require people to take action in order to reveal relevant help text when they feel they need it.

Automatic Inline Help

Automatic inline help systems reveal themselves when and where the information they contain is most applicable. For example, when a person clicks or tabs to an input field, the relevant help text appears beside or below the input. The Wufoo example in Figure 7.4 shows this behavior in action.

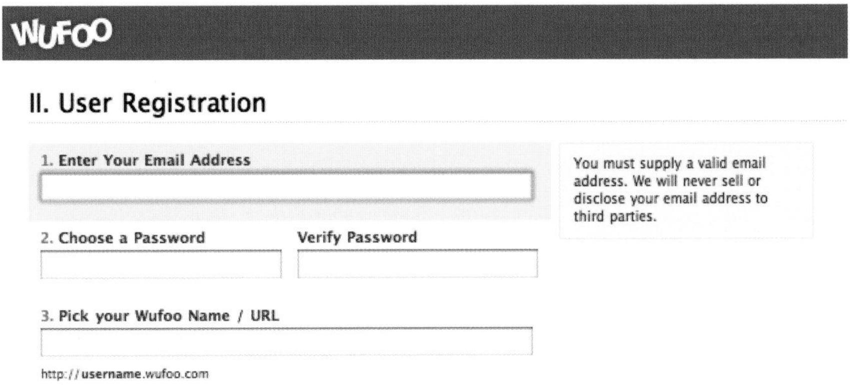

WUFOO

II. User Registration

1. Enter Your Email Address

You must supply a valid email address. We will never sell or disclose your email address to third parties.

2. Choose a Password   Verify Password

3. Pick your Wufoo Name / URL

http://username.wufoo.com

FIGURE 7.4
On Wufoo, help text is automatically shown as people engage with input fields.

In order for help text to appear in a predictable location, this approach requires an area of the Web page be dedicated to dynamic help text. In the Wufoo example, the right-hand side of the form serves this need. The advantage of this method is that help text always appears to the right of input fields. The disadvantage is that it may be disassociated from input fields all the way on the left side of the form.

The automatic inline help system used by Form Assembly in Figure 7.5 does not require a dedicated portion of the screen for displaying help text. Instead, it displays help text directly below the input field to which it applies. The advantage here is that help text is right next to the question being answered, so there's little chance of disassociation. The disadvantage, however, is that additional input fields may be covered up by help text dialogs, as seen in Figure 7.5.

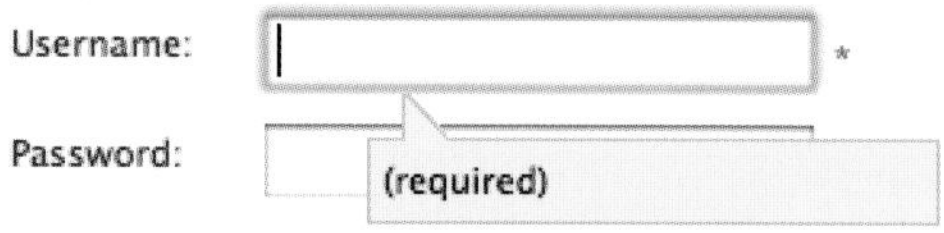

FIGURE 7.5
Here is an alternate presentation style for inline help text on Form Assembly.

Username:

Password: (required)

It's important to be as specific as possible with help text, which usually means unique help text for each individual input field. However, sometimes the most specific we can get is a set of related input fields.

When help text is more applicable to a set of related input fields than an individual input, automatic inline help can also be useful. For example, the SnapTax Web application in Figure 7.6 automatically highlights relevant information for each set of information: identity, spouse, address, and so on.

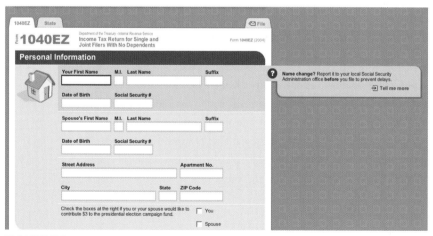

FIGURE 7.6
SnapTax automatically reveals help text for related groups of input fields.

It is worthwhile to note that all of these examples make use of a strong visual element to communicate the relationship between input fields and their associated help text. In the Wufoo example in Figure 7.4, you'll see two aligned rectangles. In the Form Assembly example in Figure 7.5, you'll notice a bold yellow color and arrow. In the SnapTax example in Figure 7.6, there is a common background color.

One potential drawback of this type of automated help system is that people are unlikely to know any help text is available until they begin to fill out the form. As a result, people who feel they may need help to complete the form might get discouraged and not even try.

A possible way to address this shortcoming is with help text within an input field. This method is essentially the opposite of automatic inline exposure because the help text is visible *before* someone accesses an input field but no longer visible *after*. Because help text is visible right away, people know help is available when they first encounter the form.

However, the only type of help text really suited for display inside an input field is help that outlines recommended ways of providing answers. Help text that explains what is being asked, why people are being asked, and whether or not questions are optional does not belong inside an input field. Figure 7.7 illustrates this principle. How the Postal Code on this form should be provided is included within the input field. Why it should be provided is explained with help text adjacent to the input field.

FIGURE 7.7

Help text within an input field on LinkedIn.

Also, the same caveats that apply to labels within input fields (discussed in Chapter 4) also apply to help text within input fields:

- Make sure the help text goes away when people are providing answers so it does not become part of their answers.

- Be aware that the help text is gone as soon as people start providing an answer so they immediately lose any assistance the help text provided.

- Be wary of using this method for complex inputs that benefit from always visible help.

- Make sure that people can tell the difference between answers in input fields and help text within input fields. In the LinkedIn example in Figure 7.7, help text is gray and includes the prefix "eg:"

Because they show no help text up front, automatic inline help systems tend to work best for forms that ask questions people are likely to have answers for but may be apprehensive or unsure about how to provide them. When specific help text needs to be provided for each input field, consider using a method that displays help adjacent to the field to which it applies. When help text is specific to a group of inputs, consider using a method that consistently displays help text in a predictable location.

User-Activated Inline Help

Another way to let people know help is available up front is with a user-activated inline help system. User-activated inline help lets people explicitly access help text when they need it. This method usually makes consistent use of an icon, button, image, or text link to let people know help is available. A person can either click or point to these triggers to reveal relevant help text as needed.

Figure 7.8 shows an example of user-activated inline help from Juicy Studios. When a person clicks on the question mark icon, an explanation of the question being asked (in this case, the IMEI Code) is revealed directly below the input field. Adding help text to a form in this manner, however, can cause content below the inserted help text to jump further down the Web page. Too much shifting of content can leave people disoriented as the form they are filling out continues to move up and down.

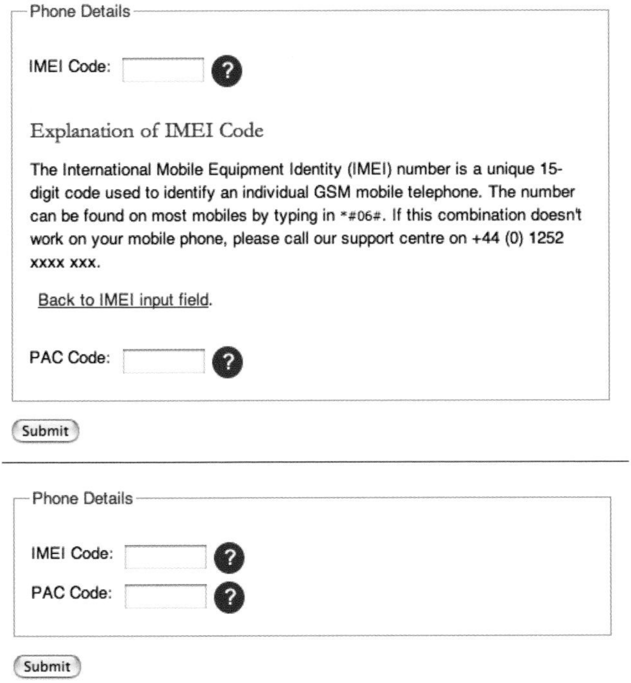

Phone Details

IMEI Code: [   ] ❓

Explanation of IMEI Code

The International Mobile Equipment Identity (IMEI) number is a unique 15-digit code used to identify an individual GSM mobile telephone. The number can be found on most mobiles by typing in *#06#. If this combination doesn't work on your mobile phone, please call our support centre on +44 (0) 1252 xxxx xxx.

Back to IMEI input field.

PAC Code: [   ] ❓

[Submit]

Phone Details

IMEI Code: [   ] ❓
PAC Code: [   ] ❓

[Submit]

FIGURE 7.8
Juicy Studios' user-activated in-line help system inserts help text within a form pushing everything down the page. This type of page "jumping" may disorient people as they complete a form.

Another drawback to the Juicy Studios implementation is the placement of the help icon next to the input field, rather than next to the label. As we saw in Chapter 5 when discussing required input field indicators, associating symbols with labels allows people to scan forms more easily for information they need.

The Wells Fargo example in Figure 7.9 addresses these two issues by making the labels themselves the triggers for help text (indicated by blue color and underlines) and surfacing help text in a small window adjacent to the link that triggered it. When the help text is placed on top of, instead of inside the form, the effects of page jumping are avoided.

However, the same caveats for automatic inline help dialogs (seen in Figure 7.5) apply here as the help text can cover up other labels or input fields when revealed, as shown in Figure 7.9.

SEC Returns	Choose from dropdown OR enter a minumum value	
1 Year Return	Any ▼	Min: [ ] %
5 Year Return	Any ▼	Min: [ ] %
10 Year Return	Any ▼	Min: [ ] %
10 Year Return The Ten-Year Return is the fund's average annualized return for the last ten years. It measures the percentage change in NAV assuming reinvestment of all dividends and capital gains.	Any ▼	Min: [ ] %
	Any ▼	
Redemption Fee	Any ▼	

FIGURE 7.9

Wells Fargo uses a small window to reveal help text when people click on each input label.

Utilizing a rollover trigger to expose help text (Figure 7.10) allows us to surface help content temporarily. Because rollover interactions require people to keep their pointers continually positioned on a trigger's hot spot to keep content visible, there are no page jumping effects, and when people move their pointer off the hot spot, the help text disappears.

The disadvantage of this method is that help content can only be seen when the pointer is deliberately positioned on a trigger's hot spot. Extending the size of the rollover's activation area is recommended to make it easier for people to trigger the help text display. Any time you're showing additional information when people roll over a hot spot, you may want to consider adding a delay of about 500 milliseconds to make sure people really wanted the help and didn't accidentally mouse over the trigger.

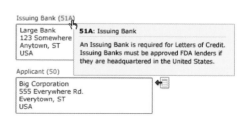

FIGURE 7.10

Help text accessed with a mouse rollover can obscure input fields as seen in this sample form QLC.

A question mark is the most common symbol for an icon that displays help content, but there are other symbols you could use (see Figure 7.11). Regardless of whether you use an icon, button, text, or a combination thereof to indicate points at which people can access help text, it's generally a good idea to include some kind of visual cue that indicates such elements are actionable—for example, a 3D bevel or underlining beneath text. It's also a good idea to place these access points next to labels rather than input fields for reasons mentioned earlier.

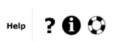

FIGURE 7.11

Though many symbols have been used to represent help, the question mark icon continues to be the most recognizable.

Forms that ask complex questions and tend to get reused by the same people are good candidates for user-activated inline help. These systems allow first-time users to access all the help they need, and advanced users to only trigger the few bits of help they require to jog their memory or answer a quick question. Because of page jumping and rollover interaction issues, I tend to favor user-activated inline help systems that surface help text on top of the form and adjacent to the label and input field to which they apply.

User-Activated Section Help

User-activated help text can also be displayed in a consistent location on a form, instead of being shown adjacent to the input fields where it applies. Making use of a consistent area where help text is displayed can provide a larger display surface for extensive help text and content such as graphics or charts and provide people with a permanent location where help text can be found.

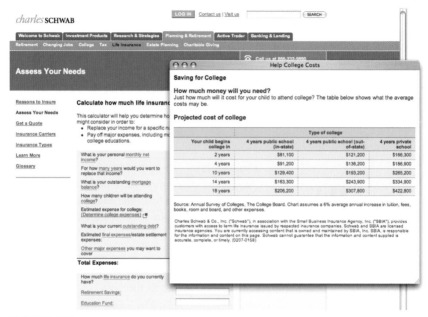

FIGURE 7.12
Charles Schwab uses a new Web browser window to show large amounts of help text, including this chart.

While many sites use a new Web browser window to display large amounts of user-activated help text (Figure 7.12), pop-up blockers and poor windowing controls sometimes make this method less than ideal. An alternative I've seen work well in testing is to utilize a consistent area adjacent to the form for contextual Help. Vizu's help section shown in Figure 7.13 does just that. A consistent column to the right of the form displays relevant help text as the form is filled in. Considering this is Vizu's registration form, though, this approach might be overkill, and Vizu may have been better off using an automatic inline help system for this form instead.

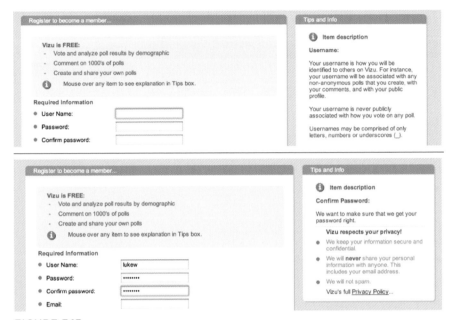

FIGURE 7.13

Vizu's help section displays help text relevant to the active input fields within a consistent location on the form.

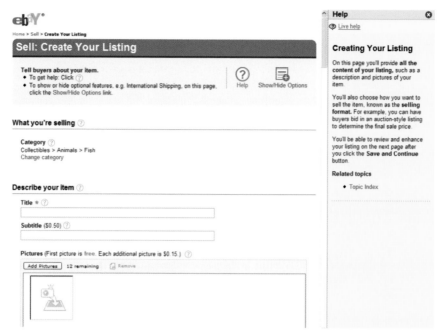

FIGURE 7.14

eBay's Sell Your Item Help panel can be turned on and off at any time.

Like user-activated inline help, user-activated section help is a better fit for forms used more than once, particularly ones that ask potentially complex questions. As such, a better candidate for this type of system is eBay's Sell Your Item form (Figure 7.14). This form makes use of a Help panel that people can display or hide by clicking a global Help icon at the top of the form. The content in the Help panel updates with contextually relevant help text when a person clicks one of the Help icons next to each input field. When open, the Help panel also automatically updates with relevant content as people move from field to field while completing the form.

So first-time sellers on eBay can simply leave the Help panel open and get detailed help as they move through the form. Advanced users can choose to close the panel and only open it when needed. The size of the panel allows eBay to include graphics, charts, and extensive help text that wouldn't fit in an inline help system.

Secure Transactions

When you're dealing with sensitive information, like credit card numbers or bank accounts, an additional bit of help text that reassures people their information is safe may be appropriate. It's important that this help text has some "meat" behind it. In other words, it should be actionable, allowing people to verify the security you promise. Many online services such as Versign or Trust-e will allow people to confirm the authenticity of a secure transaction by accessing their service from your form (see Figure 7.15).

FIGURE 7.15
Various ways of verifying a secure transaction.

If you are asking people to provide sensitive information, you may want to engage the services of one of these trusted third parties to reassure people that their data will be safe.

Best Practices

- Don't use help text to compensate for the shortcomings of your forms. Striving to minimize the amount of help text on your forms will push you toward better design solutions.

- Help text is best for explaining unfamiliar data requests, such as why certain questions are being asked, security and privacy concerns, recommended ways of providing answers, and indicating optional answers.

- Concise help text visible and adjacent to the question being asked provides the most clarity for people.

- Help text within input fields should only be used to provide recommended ways of answering questions.

- If your form is asking questions people have answers for but may be unsure how or why they should answer, consider using an automatic inline help system.

- If your form is asking unfamiliar or complex questions, and is likely to be reused by the same people multiple times, consider using a user-activated help system.

- Unless you have a lot of help text or content (graphics, charts), for each question being asked, use an inline system that avoids page-jumping and rollover problems.

- If you do have a lot of help content, use a consistent help section instead of an in-line solution.

- Be as specific as you can with help text. If help text applies to a group of related input fields instead of individual inputs, consider devoting a portion of the page to displaying help to communicate a clear association between the group of fields and the help text.

- Triggers for user-activated help text, such as icons, links, or buttons, should be placed next to labels and not input fields.

- When asking for sensitive information, consider including actionable help text that allows people to confirm that their information is safe.

Errors and Success

While help text can be used to tell people how to successfully complete a form, it isn't the most important thing we have to tell them. That honor falls to error and success messages. Error messages let people know when they cannot continue completing a form and how they can remedy the situation. Success messages tell people what they wanted to hear from the moment they starting filling in a form—they're done!

Like help text, errors and success are messages for people. As a result, a lot of the best practices and dynamic systems we looked at in Chapter 7 for help text also apply to the error and success messages discussed here.

Errors

Despite our best efforts to structure questions and input fields in meaningful ways, sometimes people will misunderstand or rush through our forms and mistakes may happen. Of course, we want to minimize the potential for these types of errors as much as we can—that's what most of this book is about! But when mistakes do happen, we should be prepared to deal with them quickly and gracefully.

Step one for dealing with errors is letting people know they happened. Though this may seem like a trivial point, all too often error messages don't get the attention they deserve. When present, an error message is arguably the most important element on the page. It prevents people from achieving their primary goal of completing a form. As a result, the visual presentation of an error needs to match its importance.

Consider the example from Fairmont Hotels in Figure 8.1. Believe it or not, there's an error preventing someone from completing this form. Let me know when you find it. And while you're at it, let me know when you find the form that led to the error!

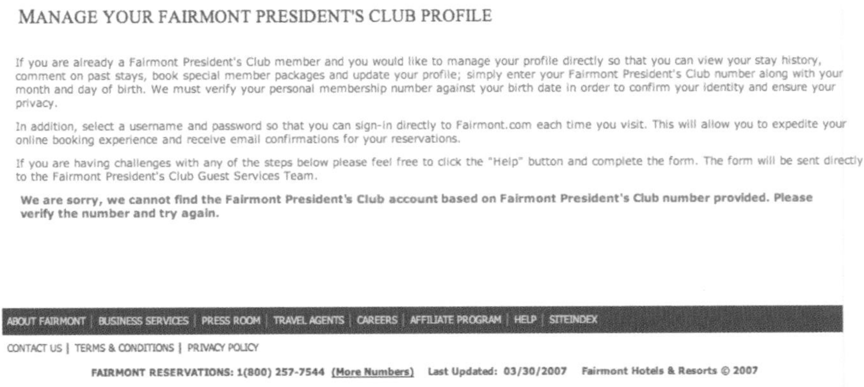

MANAGE YOUR FAIRMONT PRESIDENT'S CLUB PROFILE

If you are already a Fairmont President's Club member and you would like to manage your profile directly so that you can view your stay history, comment on past stays, book special member packages and update your profile; simply enter your Fairmont President's Club number along with your month and day of birth. We must verify your personal membership number against your birth date in order to confirm your identity and ensure your privacy.

In addition, select a username and password so that you can sign-in directly to Fairmont.com each time you visit. This will allow you to expedite your online booking experience and receive email confirmations for your reservations.

If you are having challenges with any of the steps below please feel free to click the "Help" button and complete the form. The form will be sent directly to the Fairmont President's Club Guest Services Team.

We are sorry, we cannot find the Fairmont President's Club account based on Fairmont President's Club number provided. Please verify the number and try again.

ABOUT FAIRMONT | BUSINESS SERVICES | PRESS ROOM | TRAVEL AGENTS | CAREERS | AFFILIATE PROGRAM | HELP | SITEINDEX

CONTACT US | TERMS & CONDITIONS | PRIVACY POLICY

FAIRMONT RESERVATIONS: 1(800) 257-7544 **(More Numbers)**   Last Updated: 03/30/2007   Fairmont Hotels & Resorts © 2007

FIGURE 8.1
Where's the error on this Fairmont Hotels form?

Not only is the error message comingled with three paragraphs of instructions, it is also displayed in the same font face and color as the rest of the text on the page. The only difference is that the error text is bold. No wonder you didn't notice it.

Perhaps more concerning than the visual presentation of this error message is the lack of a clear way to resolve the error itself. The message tells us to "Please verify the number and try again." But where is the number? How do I try again? Surfacing the error message next to the responsible elements would have made a solution much more understandable and actionable.

Let's consider how Fairmont Hotels could provide clear feedback that people could use to resolve this error. In the redesigned Fairmont Hotels form page in Figure 8.2, you'll notice a few things. First, there's a prominent message indicating that an error has occurred. There are several ways to distinguish important messages from the rest of a form; in this example, we've chosen a contrasting color (red), a distinct visual element (warning icon), and a prominent placement (top of the page).

Of course, you aren't limited to this exact visual presentation. Anything that has a very strong contrast with the rest of the page and looks like an error (typically red text and a warning icon) could be appropriate. Differences in size, shape, position, texture, or color can be used alone or together to create additional emphasis. The key requirement is that the error be immediately noticeable because it is blocking someone's progress.

The redesigned form also contains two clear ways to resolve the existing error. The input field that is responsible for the problem is not only visible on the page but also prominently marked. Both the top-level message and this input field have clear instructions that encourage people to either try another answer or seek help if they can't.

FIGURE 8.2
A redesigned version of the Fairmont Hotels error page makes it much clearer that there is an error preventing people from continuing.

The inclusion of instructions next to the input field responsible for the error provides people with a remedy where they need it most: where the error can be fixed. Consider an alternative where the fact that an error occurred is shown in a modal dialog window (Figure 8.3) that has to be dismissed before someone can proceed. Once that dialog is gone, so is the indication of which input needs to be corrected and how.

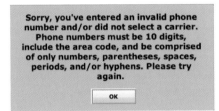

FIGURE 8.3
This error message lacks a title that associates it with an input field, is difficult to read because of the centered, bold font, and has to be remembered when dismissed. Not a very effective way to remedy errors.

In the redesigned Fairmont Hotels form (Figure 8.2), the input field responsible for the error uses a "double visual emphasis" to stand out from the rest of the form elements. In this case, the label is red, and we've added red instructions just below the input field. This doubled-up approach is important because simply changing the text color of the label might not be enough to be noticed by color-blind people. So to ensure that everyone knows where an error happened, we double the visual emphasis. We could have opted for an icon and red text or a background color and instructions to highlight the inputs responsible for the error as well. Any form of double emphasis could work, as the examples in Figure 8.4 show.

FIGURE 8.4
Several options for indicating errors with "double visual emphasis."

However, when you do decide on a visual treatment for the inputs responsible for an error, make sure that the style you select matches the style of any primary error messages on the form. Clear visual similarities between errors and error messages help people connect the dots.

Perspective: James Reffell
Director, Search User Experience, Yahoo! Inc.
Fun with Messages

Error messages aren't big-time fun for designers or customers. But dealing with them—and other forms of messaging within a form—is a critical part of the user experience, and handling them well or badly may make a huge difference in the overall success of a form.

HOW MANY TYPES OF MESSAGES?

When planning your messaging system, you have to figure out how many types of messages you'll need for your entire application—and fewer is almost always better. If you've designed a form that's so simple it doesn't have any messages, then you're a rock star! For most folks, you'll need one or two types. If you think you need three, you're edging into complexity that hurts the user (and likely the system). If you hit four or more, you've probably done something horribly wrong and should start over.

ERROR MESSAGES

Error messages are the most common, the most overused, and the most likely to annoy your customers. Avoid them where possible by using input types with no error states (such as drop-down menus), inputs that have undo options, and inputs with good default values. Where you can't avoid error messages, use them sparingly.

There are only two reasons to show an error message:

1. The customer has entered something that the system can't accept, so the customer can't continue (for example, a mismatching username and password). This kind of message should clearly and succinctly tell the customer what happened, how to fix it, and then move on.

2. Something very, very bad has happened to the system, so the customer can't continue (e.g., an essential server just got smote by lightning). This kind of message should be very apologetic and should give the customer some alternate way of contacting you.

There are no other reasons to show an error message. If you show something that looks like an error message in order to market something to the customer, you are a bad person.

SUCCESS MESSAGES

Success messages are a nice way of thanking your customer for putting up with your tedious form and its error messages. They should be short and sweet, the visual equivalent of hearing "Have a nice day!" on your way out of the grocery store.

ANY OTHER KIND OF MESSAGES

For various reasons you may be tempted to add additional kinds of messages, like the following:

- Educational messages

- Marketing messages thinly disguised as educational messages

- The "something bad has happened, and while theoretically the user could continue, it might be a bad idea" message

- Site-specific messages (e.g., "You're outbid!" on eBay)

- A clip-art picture of a mouse with a pencil (don't ask!)

Basically, you should try to avoid all of these. They introduce additional complexity, and inevitably any message that's in the squishy area of "not bad or good but somewhere in between" has a high likelihood of being misunderstood. If you must add an additional type, be very specific about when it should or should not be used, make it visually distinct from the other message types, and test the heck out of it with real users.

HOW TO BUILD GREAT MESSAGES

Once you've figured out how many types of message you have, you need to build a visual and textual framework for them. The way that messages look and sound should match your overall look and feel, have the right tone, and feel like a family of messages while being clearly distinct from each other. Messages often include icons, text, a surrounding structure, and in some cases, dynamic behavior (such as fading in). The placement and visual structure of the message should both be prominent enough to be noticed and lead the user to the part of the form that needs attention.

Perspective: James Reffell (Continued)

Good messaging icons differ from each other in multiple ways: symbol, color, and shape:

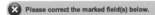

This redundancy helps people cognitively process them faster, as well as covering for things like color-blindness.

The symbols used should work well globally, as the ones here do, despite originating in Western alphabets. Other commonly used symbols can be misinterpreted in some contexts: for example, the flag icon often used as a warning icon actually connotes success in some countries. When in doubt, test—and test globally.

WHEN TO BREAK THE RULES

Of course, at the end of the day, your messages should fit your application and your customers. For business or ecommerce applications, you want clear, consistent, and friendly messages. But if you're building a crazy Web 2.0 application that's used mostly by geeks in the Bay Area to tell their friends what kind of sandwich they had for lunch and is having scaling problems, you might just do this instead:

Some cat is doing an upgrade to Twitter. Buckle your seatbelts and check back in a few!

Now, what happens when there is more than one error on a form? Or when no particular input fields are responsible for the problem, such as when a server goes down or a payment cannot be authorized? In most cases, the same structure still works well.

1. A prominent message indicating an error has happened

2. Double visual emphasis for any input fields responsible for the error (if they exist)

3. Clear explanations and actions that allow people to quickly resolve the error present in both places

The eBay Want It Now form in Figure 8.5 shows how a prominent message, double visual emphasis, and clear resolution instructions in both places could be presented when a form contains many errors.

FIGURE 8.5
A clear message and ways to resolve multiple input errors on eBay.

I've heard some designers argue that this approach creates too much clutter on a form and in cases where every input field has an active error, this can certainly be the case. However, situations like this are quite rare because most people don't provide invalid answers to *every* question when trying to complete a form.

Instead, the more common case is when one or two input fields are preventing someone from completing a form. In these instances, it is quite useful to be able to locate the responsible input field(s) quickly and easily—especially on long forms, as the example from QLC in Figure 8.6 indicates. Notice that the visual similarity (color, border, font) between the error message and responsible input fields creates a clear connection between the two.

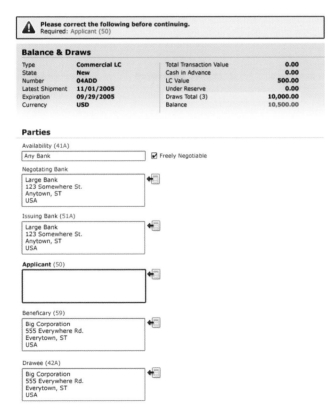

FIGURE 8.6

On long forms, such as this one from QLC, a prominent error message and double visual emphasis on invalid input fields helps people quickly notice and remedy errors.

However, there may be situations where "less is more" and a single prominent error message can do the trick. On short forms, like Figure 8.7 from Jotspot Live, a prominent message explains which input field is responsible for the error and provides a hint on how to resolve it. Personally, I feel the form could be improved with a double visual emphasis on the responsible input field so that people could find it quickly, and it could also include some additional instructions on how to remedy the error, such as "What do I do if this is my email address and it is already registered?"

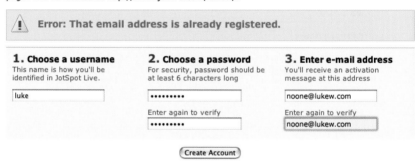

FIGURE 8.7
A single prominent message lets people know an error happened on Jotspot Live. Though how to resolve it isn't as clear.

If you do choose only to utilize a prominent message and not highlight the responsible input fields, be certain that you clearly distinguish the error message from the rest of the form. This sign-up form from Boingo in Figure 8.8 does not use enough contrast, opting instead to use the same font face and color as the form title and input labels. This makes the fact that an error happened much less obvious.

It doesn't help that Boingo has used red text for all the labels on this form, which makes it much harder to distinguish an error that is also rendered in red text. Because red text has the clearest association with errors for most people, I always recommend not using it for labels or help text to avoid any potential confusion.

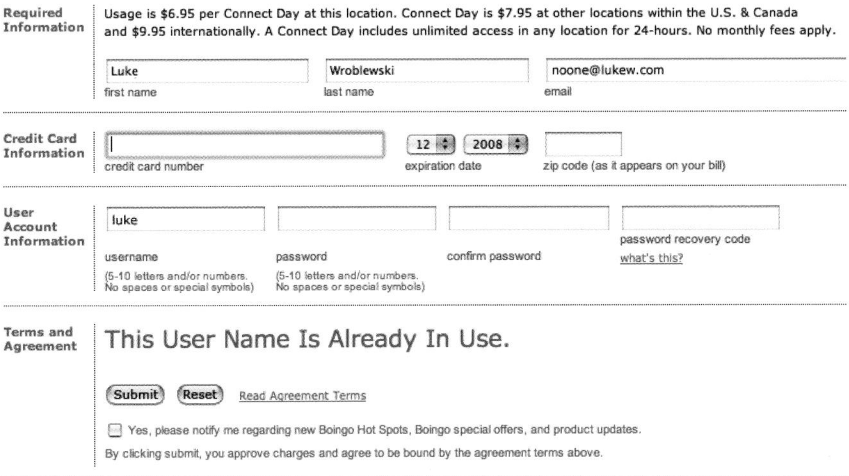

FIGURE 8.8
Boingo's error message blends in with its surroundings and, as a result, can be hard to notice.

Another potential solution for short forms is to rely on double visual emphasis for each invalid input and not utilize a top-level error message at all (see Figure 8.9). Though this may work with shorter forms, it could create issues on longer forms when the responsible input fields appear offscreen because they are "below the fold" of a monitor's viewable area. In such cases, people might have a hard time knowing an error is blocking their progress.

One potential way to address this is to jump to the point of the first error on a form. That way, the first thing someone sees is an input field that needs to be corrected. When multiple input fields are invalid, however, this method doesn't give people an overview of all the errors present on the form. They are simply taken to the first and may or may not know others exist. A top-level error message, on the other hand, could clearly list all the errors that need to be addressed before someone can proceed.

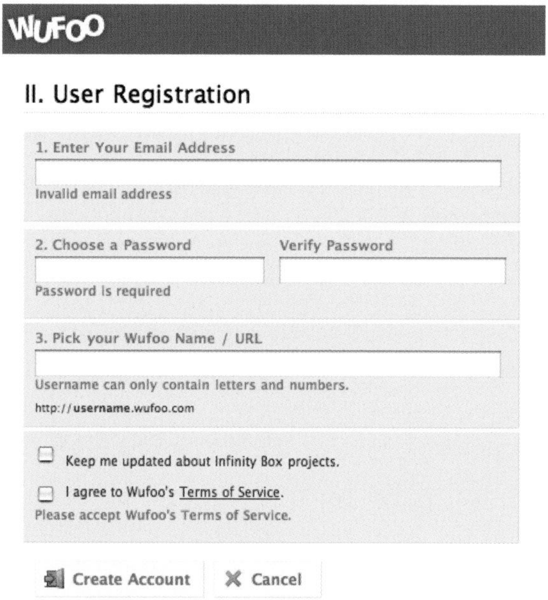

FIGURE 8.9
On this short form, Wufoo does not utilize a top-level message and instead embeds instructions on how to remedy each error with each input field. Distinguishing the label from remedy instructions (right now both are bold) could help make these errors easier to scan.

Success

Finally, the moment we've all been waiting for. Someone completes our form with no errors. Success!

But now what?

Before we get ahead of ourselves, let's make sure people know they've hit this milestone. They answered all our carefully selected questions using the input fields we provided. So how about a pat on the back? Think of success messages as just that—a way to let people know they accomplished their goal. They became a customer, they added or edited their data, they bought the item they wanted. Congrats.

Although not as important as an error message, a success message should be noticeable enough to give people the quick praise they deserve. As a result, many of the distinctions that applied to error messages can also work for success messages: different colors, shapes, fonts, sizes, and more. The key difference between error and success messages, however, is that error messages cannot be ignored or dismissed—they must be addressed. Success messages, on the other hand, should never block people's progress—they should encourage more of it.

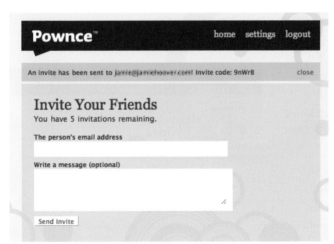

FIGURE 8.10
Pownce uses a short success message that does not get in the way of further action and clearly explains the result of people's actions.

The success message on Pownce's Invite Your Friends form in Figure 8.10 provides a noticeable confirmation that a form was completed successfully. The message is shown in context on the same form that was just completed. This context is probably appropriate because someone who just invited a friend is likely to want to invite additional friends. The success message doesn't get in the way. In fact, it even provides a way to get out of the way by including a link to close the message and remove it from the page.

Pownce's success message contains information that people can use to confirm their intended actions took place. It not only tells you that an invite was set, it specifies to whom, and it provides a way to access that information again (with an invite code). That's valuable information to keep visible on the screen. In other cases, the only confirmation needed is that a form was completed successfully or that an action took place. In these situations, it may be appropriate to automatically remove success messages, preferably with animation.

Because human beings are instinctively drawn to motion—we had to avoid saber-toothed tigers somehow—animated messages that transition off a page can let people know their actions have been successful. The most common transitions utilized for this are fades, dissolves, or roll-ups.

In 37signal's project management application, Basecamp (Figure 8.11), when a new message is created—by filling in a form, of course, people are taken to a list of existing messages where an animation indicates where the message they created appears. This context is appropriate for this action because people just added a message to this list. That's where they can read it, edit it, delete, and comment on it.

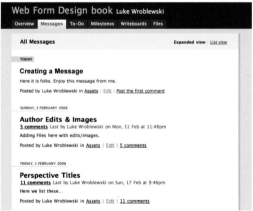

In other situations, the most appropriate context may actually be the form someone just filled in. For a records database of customer information, providing a success message on the form that your customer just updated gives

FIGURE 8.11
When you are adding a new message to Basecamp, a fading background color around your addition lets you know you have been successful.

that person an opportunity to review changes, make other changes, or locate other records to update.

No Dead Ends

Success messages can also include useful follow-up actions related to the task someone just completed (see Figure 8.12). Booked a flight online? Perhaps you want to forward your itinerary to family? Making these actions part of a success message on the page gives people clear and actionable next steps. Never leave 'em hanging!

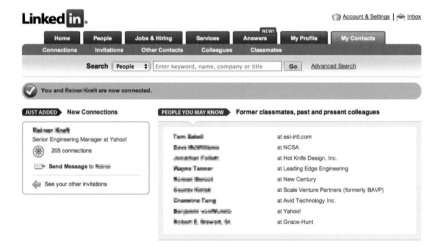

FIGURE 8.12
After you have connected with someone on the professional networking site LinkedIn, the success page provides several relevant next steps.

Best Practices

- Clearly communicate when an error is blocking someone from completing a form. Error messages are arguably the most important element on a form when present. Make sure they appear that way!

- Display error messages in context so they can be resolved quickly.

- Provide actionable remedies that enable people to resolve errors easily.

- Top-level error messages should indicate an error has occurred and how it can be resolved. If multiple errors exist, they should be listed in the top-level message.

- If any input fields are responsible for an error, clearly mark them with a double visual emphasis to ensure they are noticeable.

- Visually associate any responsible form elements with a top-level error message to clearly communicate they need to be resolved in order to continue.

- Reserve red text and warning icons for error messages.

- On short forms, it may be possible to omit either a top-level message or indicators for responsible input fields. If you choose this approach—do so thoughtfully.

- Clearly communicate when a form has been completed successfully and what happened as a result using success messages.

- Provide success messages in context so as not to block any further progress.

- Consider dynamic success messages to highlight the results of a successful form submission.

- Avoid success message page dead ends.

Inline Validation

Despite our best efforts to format questions clearly and provide meaningful affordances for our inputs, some of our questions will always have more than one possible answer. In these cases, direct feedback can help reassure people that their answers are valid. This type of real-time communication is often implemented as inline validation.

Inline validation can provide several types of feedback: confirmation that an appropriate answer was given, suggestions for valid answers, and real-time updates designed to help people stay within necessary limits. These bits of feedback usually happen when people begin, continue, or stop entering answers within input fields.

Confirmation

Confirming appropriate answers is most useful when there is a high likelihood that people won't get the answer "right." A common example is the selection of a unique username. Chances are good that the first username to pop into people's heads is one that someone else already claimed. Providing that specific answer would yield an error because the Web site understands that it is not "valid." Someone else already has that username. Of course, it's impossible for people to know what usernames are available to them when they are filling in a registration form so they continue to guess and guess again until they stumble upon something obscure enough not to be taken.

This situation becomes worse when the form does nothing to help. In the Boingo example in Figure 9.1, not only is there no feedback that helps people pick a valid answer, but the feedback that tells them an error occurred is hard to even notice as it uses the same font face and color as the form's labels (see Chapter 8 for more on error messages).

| Required Information | Usage is $6.95 per Connect Day at this location. Connect Day is $7.95 at other locations within the U.S. & Canada and $9.95 internationally. A Connect Day includes unlimited access in any location for 24-hours. No monthly fees apply. |

| | Luke | Wroblewski | noone@lukew.com |
| | first name | last name | email |

| Credit Card Information | 333444555666 | 12 ⬍ 2008 ⬍ | 55555 |
| | credit card number | expiration date | zip code (as it appears on your bill) |

User Account Information	lukew	••••••	••••••	
	username	password	confirm password	password recovery code
	(5-10 letters and/or numbers. No spaces or special symbols)	(5-10 letters and/or numbers. No spaces or special symbols)		what's this?

Terms and Agreement	(Submit) (Reset) Read Agreement Terms
	☐ Yes, please notify me regarding new Boingo Hot Spots, Boingo special offers, and product updates.
	By clicking submit, you approve charges and agree to be bound by the agreement terms above.

| Required Information | Usage is $6.95 per Connect Day at this location. Connect Day is $7.95 at other locations within the U.S. & Canada and $9.95 internationally. A Connect Day includes unlimited access in any location for 24-hours. No monthly fees apply. |

| | Luke | Wroblewski | noone@lukew.com |
| | first name | last name | email |

| Credit Card Information | 333444555666 | 12 ⬍ 2008 ⬍ | 55555 |
| | credit card number | expiration date | zip code (as it appears on your bill) |

User Account Information	lukew			
	username	password	confirm password	password recovery code
	(5-10 letters and/or numbers. No spaces or special symbols)	(5-10 letters and/or numbers. No spaces or special symbols)		what's this?

Terms and Agreement	## This User Name Is Already In Use.
	(Submit) (Reset) Read Agreement Terms
	☐ Yes, please notify me regarding new Boingo Hot Spots, Boingo special offers, and product updates.
	By clicking submit, you approve charges and agree to be bound by the agreement terms above.

FIGURE 9.1

In the Boingo sign-up form, people bounce back and forth trying to guess a valid username.

An alternate approach can be seen on the Newsvine site in Figure 9.2. Here, a simple snippet of inline validation provides valuable feedback that tells people if they've entered a valid answer. Start typing and a message appears telling you if the username you selected is taken or not. When you provide a valid answer, the message updates to reflect that. In this approach, people are not left cycling between errors—they know right away if their answer is valid or not.

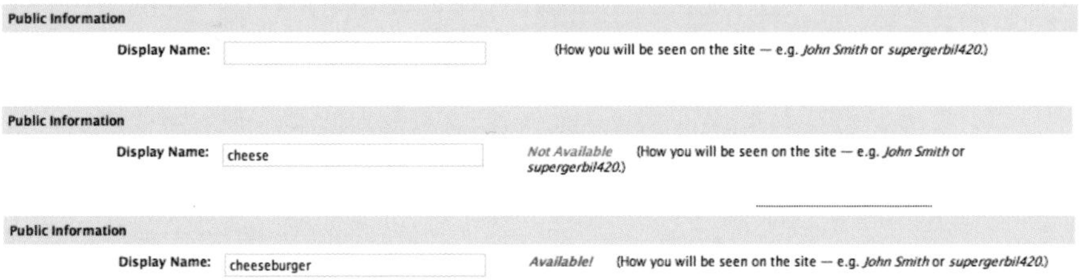

FIGURE 9.2
The Newsvine sign-up form uses inline validation to get people to an appropriate display name quickly and without pogo-sticking between error states.

Another question commonly fraught with errors is the password. I won't dwell on the fact that asking people to generate complex combinations of uppercase and lowercase letters, numerals, and symbols is another example of how our "inside out" systems create confusion for people. Instead, I'll provide a way we can help people overcome those obstacles through the use of inline validation.

When we talked about usernames, a valid answer was pretty black and white. It's either a unique username or it's not. Passwords, and other questions like them, can have varying degrees of "right." A password that meets the minimum requirements for security—say one uppercase letter and one numeral—is a valid answer. However, it is not as secure as a password with one uppercase letter, two symbols, and three numerals. The latter answer is more "right." So how can you steer people toward the more secure—and therefore right answers?

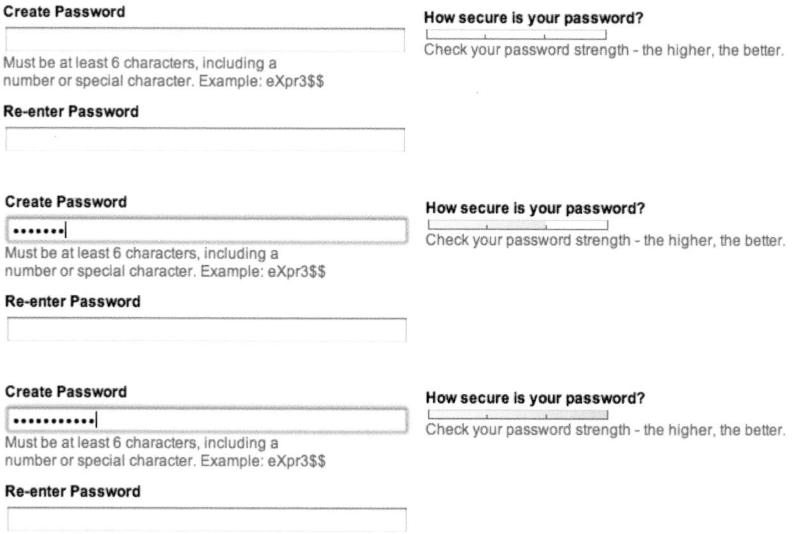

Create Password

_____

Must be at least 6 characters, including a
number or special character. Example: eXpr3$$

Re-enter Password

_____

How secure is your password?

Check your password strength - the higher, the better.

Create Password

| ••••••| |

Must be at least 6 characters, including a
number or special character. Example: eXpr3$$

Re-enter Password

_____

How secure is your password?

Check your password strength - the higher, the better.

Create Password

| ••••••••••| |

Must be at least 6 characters, including a
number or special character. Example: eXpr3$$

Re-enter Password

_____

How secure is your password?

Check your password strength - the higher, the better.

FIGURE 9.3
On eBay Express, a progress bar indicates how secure your password is in real
time.

As the eBay Express example in Figure 9.3 shows, you can utilize inline
validation not only to confirm an appropriate password has been provided
but also to indicate how appropriate that password is. The password meter
to the right of this input field gives people a highly visual way to gauge
the quality of their answer. Perhaps more importantly, it also helps ensure
that people pay attention to how they are answering this question. When
presented with a meter of this type, people are strangely compelled to
complete it. As a result, they put more thought into their answers. In this
specific example, they may end up with a password so secure they can't
remember it, but that's a different problem!

Given the benefits of confirming appropriate answers in real time, you
might be tempted to consider using inline validation for all the questions
you pose in your forms. After all, why not let people know every question
they've answered is right as they answer it? By the time they complete the
form, there's no chance of an error!

Sign up for Last.fm

Desired username:

(max 15 characters, no spaces)

Email:

☐ The occasional newsletter to keep me up-to-date.

Password:

Confirm password:

Sign up for Last.fm

Desired username: | lukew | ❗

(Try another name)

(max 15 characters, no spaces)

Email: | mail@mail.com | ✓

☐ The occasional newsletter to keep me up-to-date.

Password: | • | ❗

Confirm password: | •••• | ❗

FIGURE 9.4
Lastfm.com uses inline validation on almost every input field in its sign-up form.

I've heard arguments for and against this approach illustrated in Figure 9.4. On the one hand, validating all input fields in real time ensures that a form is completed correctly the first time through. On the other hand, validating everything could not only become a distraction, it could also raise some eyebrows.

Does validating an email address mean that it is, in fact, an email address (based on its formatting), or that it is *my* email address (and this site knows that somehow), or that this email address is already known to the site (especially important if I am registering or updating a customer record)? Though not everyone will think this way, why make people think at all? Use inline validation to help people with answers they aren't guaranteed to know. I know my name, so there's no need to validate it for me!

If you do choose to provide inline validation for many of the questions you ask, timing is everything. The Mint sign-up form in Figure 9.5 brings up an error state immediately when someone begins providing an answer. In the example illustrated, I've only managed to enter the first letter of my email address, and I'm already faced with an error. A much better approach is to only provide feedback when it's clear someone is done providing an answer. Figure 9.6 illustrates this sequence when someone completes his or her answer on the Yahoo! registration form.

FIGURE 9.5
Mint's registration form interrupts people when they are answering questions with immediate error messages.

FIGURE 9.6
Yahoo!'s registration form only validates an answer once someone has indicated he or she is done by moving to the next input field.

Suggestions

Direct feedback isn't just limited to confirming the answers I provide, but it can also be used to suggest valid answers. In situations where there's a specific set of answers that are valid but that set is too broad to fit into a single user interface element like a drop-down menu or series of radio buttons, inline suggestions can help get people to the right answer.

Quick, what's the airport code for Chicago, IL? Perhaps you knew the answer was ORD, perhaps you didn't. In either case, the inline suggestions on Kayak help ensure you provide the right answer when you are trying to travel to the Windy City. Simply start typing "chi" or "ord," and a list of valid answers you can choose from appears in Figure 9.7.

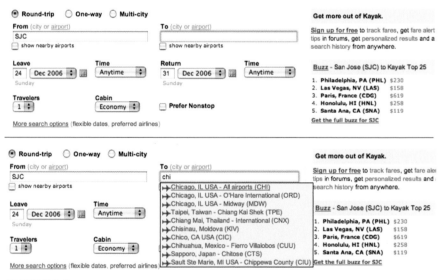

FIGURE 9.7
Kayak.com uses inline suggestions to help people provide valid answers for travel destinations.

Compared to inline confirmation, this is a different way to ensure that people provide valid answers. Instead of real-time answers that say "yes, this is valid" or "no, it is not," inline suggestions state "here are some valid answers to pick from." To further illustrate this difference, let's look again at selecting a username.

In contrast to Newsvine's approach to confirming the username people select inline (Figure 9.2), Yahoo! provides a list of valid username suggestions based on the full name that people provided earlier in the form (Figure 9.8). I entered my name as "Luke Wroblewski" at the start of the form and received several relevant, valid answers to choose from.

2. Select an ID and password

Yahoo! ID and Email [ ] @yahoo.com

These Yahoo! IDs are available: Prev | Next
5. Wroblewski_Luke 6. Luke_Wroblewski0
7. LukeW 8. WroblewskiLuke5

Password [ ]

Re-type Password [ ]

FIGURE 9.8
Yahoo!'s registration form provides a series of valid usernames based on your name.

Another alternative to suggesting valid inputs is simply making people's inputs valid whether they like it or not. Consider an input field that requires people to provide their phone number in a specific format like (XXX)-XXX-XXXX. As I mentioned in Chapter 5, we should simply accept multiple formats for this basic input, but for now let's assume we need this specific type of format.

If people enter a valid phone number in a different format, we can simply change their answer to the correct one. It's crucial that this change does not happen *while* people are actually entering their answers. Instead it should happen *after* they are done.

Limits

For questions without clearly defined answers but clearly defined limits, inline validation also comes in handy. The Yahoo! Local form in Figure 9.9 allows people to send an email to friends or family. To avoid spam or excessively long content, Yahoo! limits the message input to 1,000 characters. As people enter their answers, the counter below the input field provides real-time updates on how much more they can type.

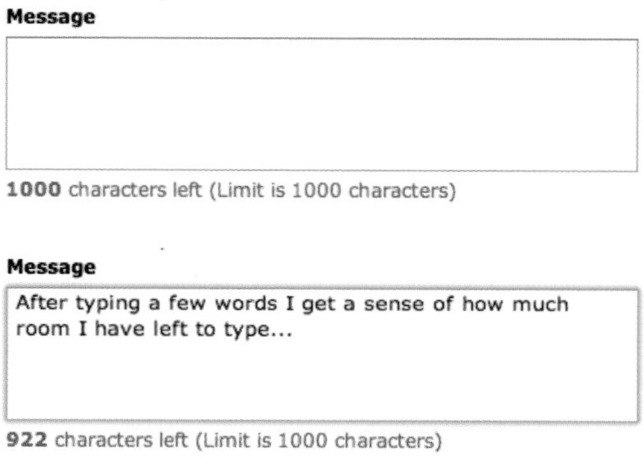

Message

1000 characters left (Limit is 1000 characters)

Message

After typing a few words I get a sense of how much room I have left to type...

922 characters left (Limit is 1000 characters)

FIGURE 9.9
Inline validation can be used to communicate limits, such as the number of characters that can be included in this message on Yahoo! Local.

This type of inline validation helps avoid potential errors if people were to exceed the limits of the input field. It's important to note that the Yahoo! character count updates immediately as you type. Any significant delay would limit the usefulness of this feature.

Best Practices

- Consider using inline validation to confirm or suggest valid answers and to help people stay within limits.

- Inline confirmation works best for questions with potentially high error rates or specific formatting requirements.

- Inline suggestions work best when there is a large set of valid answers people can pick from.

- Inline quality indicators can guide people to better answers to complex questions.

- When validating people's answers inline, do so after they have finished providing an answer, not during the process.

- If you need to change people's responses into a specific format, make sure you do so after they have finished providing an answer, not during the process.

- When input limits exist, communicate their boundaries using real-time, dynamic updates.

Unnecessary Inputs

Any question you ask people requires them to parse it, formulate a response, and then input their answer in the affordance you have provided on the form. Being vigilant about every question you ask allows you to remove questions that are not absolutely necessary, or can be asked at a better time or place, or can be inferred automatically. And the fewer questions you ask, the better the odds are of people completing your forms quickly and easily.

Removing Questions

When eBay Inc. redesigned its registration form in 2002, the company carefully considered each question and decided which ones were not absolutely necessary. It's probably not a coincidence that some of these were also the same questions that tripped up potential customers: annual household income, gender, promotional codes, and date of birth (Figure 10.1).

Moving several optional questions out of the registration form probably required some negotiation with the people vested in their answers—marketing and trust and safety teams at the company. The impact, however, was tremendous because a lot more people registered successfully and began to use eBay. And perhaps ironically, significantly more people answered the optional questions when they were asked after they registered!

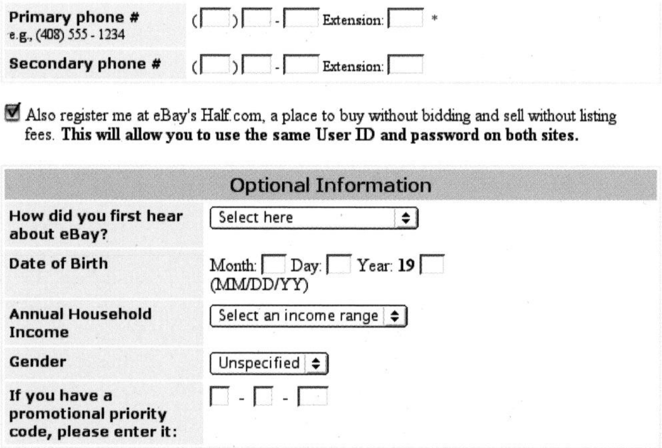
Primary phone #
e.g., (408) 555 - 1234
( ) - Extension: *
Secondary phone #
( ) - Extension:

Also register me at eBay's Half.com, a place to buy without bidding and sell without listing fees. **This will allow you to use the same User ID and password on both sites.**

Optional Information

How did you first hear about eBay? Select here

Date of Birth Month: Day: Year: 19 (MM/DD/YY)

Annual Household Income Select an income range

Gender Unspecified

If you have a promotional priority code, please enter it: - -

FIGURE 10.1 eBay's old registration form asked a number of questions that tripped up potential customers.

Of course, not all questions on a form are unnecessary. But even when you've put in the effort to make sure that everything you are asking people is, in fact, required to meet user needs or business goals, there may still be an opportunity to trim unnecessary input fields.

PayPal's payment form looks like a typical set of questions that require an answer when someone is trying to make a purchase online (Figure 10.2). People are asked to select the type of credit card they are using to pay and then provide the number for that card.

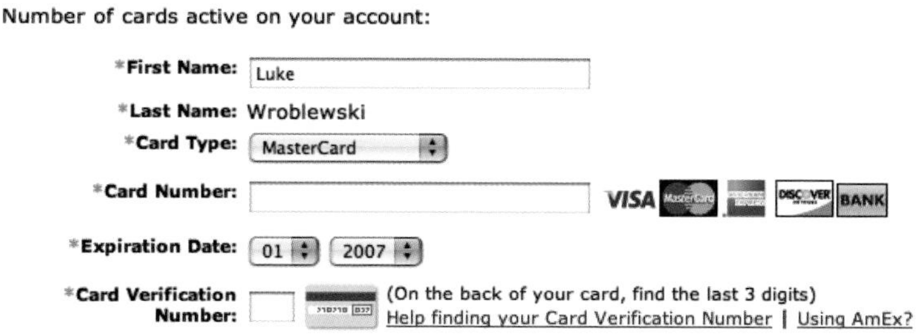

Number of cards active on your account:

*First Name:	Luke
*Last Name:	Wroblewski
*Card Type:	MasterCard
*Card Number:	VISA MasterCard DISCOVER BANK
*Expiration Date:	01 2007
*Card Verification Number:	(On the back of your card, find the last 3 digits) Help finding your Card Verification Number	Using AmEx?

FIGURE 10.2
This PayPal form asks people to select the type of credit card they are using to make a purchase. Is that necessary?

However, it turns out one of these questions is unnecessary. Credit card numbers follow a consistent structure. American Express cards start with either 34 or 37. Mastercard numbers begin with 51–55. Visa cards start with 4. And so on. This information can be used to infer what type of credit card someone is using simply by looking at his credit card number.

In the redesigned form in Figure 10.3, PayPal does exactly that. When someone enters a credit card number, the appropriate card type is highlighted directly below. This eliminates the need to ask people what type of credit card they have—one less question to parse, think through, and respond to.

FIGURE 10.3
The redesigned PayPal form eliminates an unnecessary question by highlighting the type of credit card being used.

When you are looking for ways to reduce unnecessary inputs, it's important to think through a number of considerations. In the PayPal example, the four kinds of credit cards PayPal accepts all follow a consistent numbering system, so the interaction works.

On the Weber checkout form in Figure 10.4, people are asked for their zip code first and then given a set of choices for their city and state. On the plus side, this interaction design removes some awkward ways of answering questions—specifically, drop-down menus for states that run 50 entries high.

On the negative side, the way a simple question is asked has been made more complicated. When faced with a set of input fields that match the structure of a mailing address, people often skip over labels as they fill in the pieces. The components and layout of a U.S. mailing address are familiar to just about everyone in the United States. The Weber site breaks this structure by asking for the zip code out of order.

It also removes the redundancy inherent in asking people for a zip code *and* city/state. The United States Postal Services has deliberately *not* removed these fields from mailing labels precisely because people often mistype one or the other.

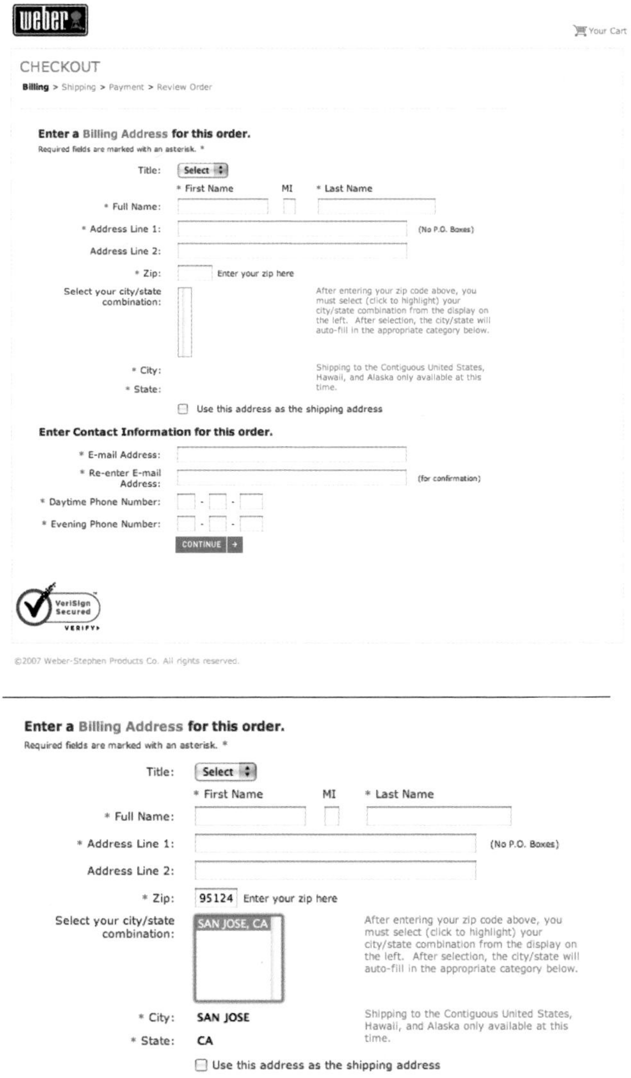

FIGURE 10.4
Weber's checkout
form tries
to eliminate
questions, but
potentially ends up
complicating the
form more.

Another indicator that the question being asked has gotten more
complicated is the extensive help text (rendered in red text) near the city
and state selection. Odds are that Weber had to add this to help people
understand what to expect from the form. The company also probably
made the help text red so people would notice it since most people pass

over instructional text when filling in forms unless they feel they need it. Trying to draw attention to help text in this way is not advised, as red text for anything but errors should be avoided.

International customers are also out of luck because Weber does not ship overseas. If it did, clearly this interaction would not work when specifying international addresses that do not utilize the United States zip code system.

So although the Weber example removes some unnecessary inputs, I think the jury is still out on whether this simplified the form or not.

Smart Defaults

In *The Paradox of Choice,*[1] author Barry Schwartz discusses the impact of having too many choices in our lives and suggests some strategies for coping with the excessive options we encounter just about everywhere. In particular, he outlines the power of smart defaults—selections put in place that serve the interests of most people—as a way to help people make good choices.

Schwartz references organ donor programs as an example. In the United States, 90 percent of Americans approve of organ donation but only 25 percent are organ donors. In several European countries, over 80 percent of people are donors. The difference comes down to a default choice. In the U.S., the organ donor option is defaulted off. Elsewhere, it is defaulted on.

There are many opportunities within Web forms to utilize the power of smart defaults to reduce the number of choices people have to make and thereby expedite form completion.

In the shipping costs portion of eBay's "sell your item" form (see Figure 10.5), three default choices are made for sellers: standard delivery, insurance not offered, and sales tax not charged. Because these choices result in the least amount of overhead for most sellers on eBay, they are smart defaults that simplify the decision-making process. Not sure what shipping service

---

[1] Barry Schwartz, *Paradox of Choice*, 2004. Harper Perennial

to use? Standard delivery is the most common. Don't know if you need to charge sales tax? Looks like you don't have to. Smart defaults provide answers to questions for you.

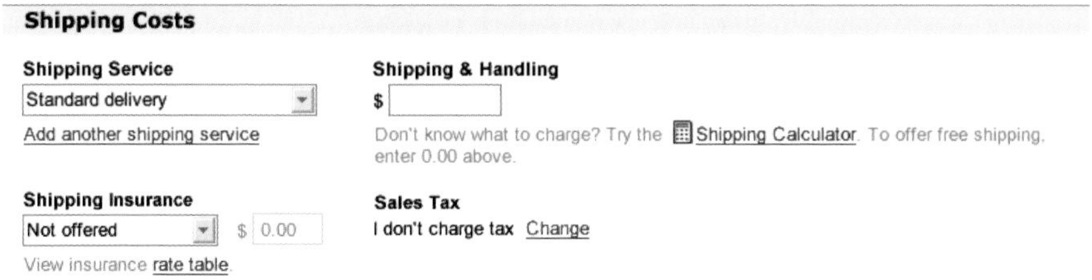

Shipping Costs

Shipping Service
Standard delivery ▼
Add another shipping service

Shipping & Handling
$ [   ]
Don't know what to charge? Try the ▦ Shipping Calculator. To offer free shipping, enter 0.00 above.

Shipping Insurance
Not offered ▼ $ 0.00
View insurance rate table.

Sales Tax
I don't charge tax Change

FIGURE 10.5
Smart defaults on the eBay "sell your item" form include answers for shipping service, insurance, and sales tax.

Because of the power of smart defaults, it is tempting to opt people into situations advantageous for business but potentially less so for customers. For example, it's common to encounter forms that opt customers into mailing lists or extra features by default (see Figure 10.6).

☑ Show my real name.
☑ Send me updates on events, news, or special announcements.
☑ Keep me informed about additional products or services.

[Create Account]

FIGURE 10.6
This form defaults people into showing their real name and getting marketing materials from the site and third parties.

If possible, try to ensure that the defaults you include in forms align with your customers' interests. When people are defaulted into services or options they don't like, it casts doubt and suspicion on your service. I've seen several instances where a default choice made potential customers wary enough to pack up their bags and not complete a form.

Perhaps the simplest form of a default selection is a preselected option within a set of radio buttons. Where appropriate, give some thought to what that initial selection is and whether or not it is the right choice for the majority of people encountering your form. Because of the power of smart defaults, chances are that many people will stick with that option.

To address this behavior, a lot of radio button inputs don't include an initial selection (see Figure 10.7). Either the form designers aren't sure what the right default should be, or they want people to explicitly make a selection.

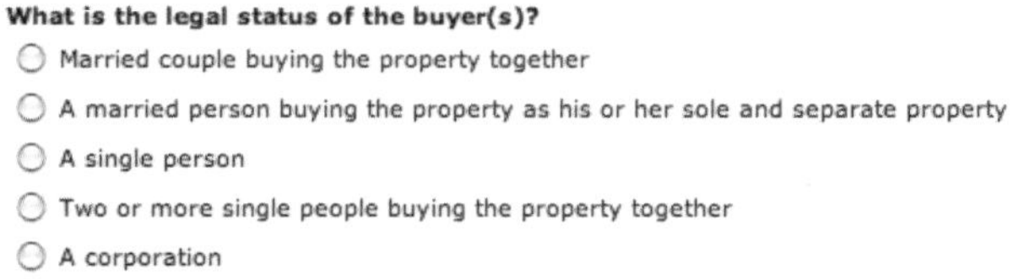

FIGURE 10.7

A set of radio buttons without an initially selected option on Redfin.

What is the legal status of the buyer(s)?
- Married couple buying the property together
- A married person buying the property as his or her sole and separate property
- A single person
- Two or more single people buying the property together
- A corporation

Interaction designers would argue that this breaks the model of a mutually exclusive interaction element. After all, a set of radio buttons without an explicit selection will result in an error when a form is submitted. While this is true, people successfully make selections from sets of radio buttons without a default choice all the time. And mutually exclusive choices exist where no default option makes sense.

Consider the question of gender: male or female (see Figure 10.8)? A radio button input is hard-pressed to select a default value without sounding presumptuous. A drop-down menu with a third "Please select" option increases the number of steps needed to answer this simple question: click on the menu, drag the mouse to select a choice, let go of the mouse. Simply clicking a radio button is much easier. Perhaps the way to get the best of both worlds is by using a drop-down menu with a third option: "rather not say." This way you're not being overly pushy!

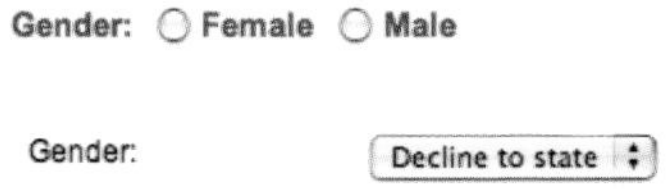

Gender: ○ Female ○ Male

FIGURE 10.8

What's the right default state for gender?

Gender: [Decline to state ⇕]

Smart defaults don't work very well when there isn't a clear option that applies to most people. The Vox registration form in Figure 10.9 defaults the birth date to Jan 1, 1975—probably not the birthday of everyone who tries to register for the site. A better solution simply would be to ask people to explicitly select the month, day, and year they were born. And while you're at it, let them know why you are asking. eBay in Figure 10.9 tells you that it isn't being nosey; you just can't sell on eBay unless you are 18.

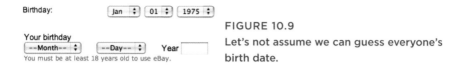

FIGURE 10.9
Let's not assume we can guess everyone's birth date.

Smart defaults can also come from people's implicit behaviors. For instance, if you know someone is accessing your form from the United States, you might consider defaulting the "Country" input field to "United States." If you know that 90 percent of your customers live in the U.S., you might do the same.

Personalized Defaults

Smart defaults can also be personally relevant to individuals. For instance, if I always use Federal Express as my Shipping Service when I sell items on eBay, the Shipping Service selection we saw earlier could be defaulted to my personal choice. Keeping selections active for returning customers is often referred to as making them "sticky," which basically means sticking with the choice a customer made before.

Though some forms set a high bar for how many times a choice must be made in order to become "sticky," many only require a single time through to set a personalized default. Expedia, for example, sets my default travel options to the last set of tickets I looked for (see Figure 10.10). The form

FIGURE 10.10
Smart defaults for travel options on the Expedia site, based on previous usage.

could be even smarter if it defaulted to my last set of travel options only until it knew I bought a ticket for that trip. In all other cases, it could simply default to my most frequently used departure airport.

Best Practices

- Carefully examine all the questions being asked in your form for opportunities to eliminate unnecessary inputs.

- Look for patterns in how people answer questions that allow you to infer answers accurately.

- Be mindful not to complicate questions for the sake of removing inputs.

- Smart defaults can help people answer questions by putting default selections in place that serve the interests of most people.

- Because people are likely to leave default selections in place, ensure they align with most people's goals.

- Whenever possible, include a default selection in a set of radio buttons. If no clear default exists, chances are that people will still understand they need to make a choice. But if they don't, they'll get an error.

- Personally relevant default selections enable return customers to complete forms faster because their answers are "sticky."

- Think through where personalized defaults make sense. It won't be every input on every form.

Additional Inputs

Not all people require all the input fields within a form at all times. There are many cases where a few simple options cover the majority of people's needs. For the remaining cases, we can turn to additional inputs: inline additions, overlays, and progressive engagement.

Inline Additions

Inline additions provide additional input fields to the people that need them without getting in the way of people that don't. These input fields are often thought of as advanced or additional options, but they don't have to be any more complicated than a normal set of choices presented in the form by default.

Let's look at a simple example. Most of the people filling out the team building form in Figure 11.1 will have only one manager. In that case, they simply enter their manager's first and last name and move on. A small number of people, most likely fewer than 10 percent, will have more than one manager. These folks can select "Add another manager" to expose input fields for multiple managers. Once they do so, they have the option to remove these additional input fields easily. The original input field, however, cannot be removed. Everyone filling in the form has at least one manager, and the inline additions don't get in the way of that primary task.

FIGURE 11.1

Adding a varying number of managers to a form doesn't have to trip up people with only one manager.

Another example can be found in the project management application, Basecamp (Figures 11.2 and 11.3). In this application, the form for creating a new message features two examples of inline additions. If people need to attach a file or a milestone to the message they are authoring, they can expose additional input fields that enable them to do so with a single click. People that don't need these features can simply ignore the links that expose them and continue on with the form.

It's probably worth noting that in both of the examples we have seen so far, the links to expose inline additions have been clearly worded so their functionality is clear: Attach files to this message, add another manager.

FIGURES 11.2 & 11.3
Exposing additional inline options in Basecamp is triggered by well-labeled links.

In the Basecamp example, inline additions are exposed below the action that triggers them, and a clear way to remove the options is provided: a visible link labeled "Cancel." Other forms of inline additions may expose input fields to the right or above the actions that triggered them to avoid too much page "jumping" when new content is added to the form.

Page jumping pushes existing content down the form and can sometimes disrupt people's awareness of their position on the page. As a result, it's always a good idea to try and minimize the amount of page jumping within a form. When using inline additions that expose additional input fields below an action, try to avoid very large sets of input fields that will push the content on a Web page down substantially. When you have a lot of additional options, exposing them to the side or in an overlay might be a better option.

Overlays

Another way to display additional options is to use an overlay: a set of additional input fields that sits on top of a form like a dialog window on your computer's desktop. Perhaps the most common example of these is the calendar widget that allows people to select specific dates as answers to questions posed by a form.

The sample form Kayak in Figure 11.4 shows up automatically when the date field is active and provides two months' worth of dates to choose from. Clearly including all these dates on the form would have added a lot of noise—it's much better to surface these options only when they are needed.

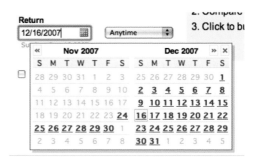

FIGURE 11.4
The date picker on Kayak is an example of an overlay that provides quick access to a lot of options.

Because many trips are likely to span a week or more, Kayak's overlay intentionally surfaces two months' worth of dates. This makes it easier for people to access the options they need. Orbitz (Figure 11.5), on the other hand, only brings up one month of options at a time, causing people to scroll month by month to find the date they need. Since Orbitz has gone through the trouble of coding and surfacing this overlay, why not take advantage of the added space and give people more useful options to pick from?

FIGURE 11.5
Only one month's worth of dates shows up in the Orbitz date selector.

In both the Orbitz and Kayak examples, the date selection options are surfaced automatically when someone places his cursor in the appropriate input field. However, only Kayak provides an indicator that this will happen by including a small calendar icon within the input field (Figure 11.4). This visual cue helps to set expectations that a calendar will be made available. And while both the Orbitz and Kayak input fields still allow people to enter a date without using the calendar overlay, the Kayak overlay does not cover the input field and thereby gets in people's way when they do so.

Where additional options are clearly useful—like the travel dates example we just looked at—automatically displaying the additional options in an overlay may be beneficial. In many other situations, a form designer's attempt to cleverly surface additional options might be met with confusion or annoyance. Most additional options are best left "user-activated," meaning they give people filling in the form the option of whether or not they see and utilize additional input fields.

Incidentally, calendar overlays on travel Web sites did not always open automatically like they do today. Each site used to have an explicit control (usually a calendar icon) for hiding and showing these elements (see Figure 11.6). Only as people's needs and behaviors came to be better understood and technology became more dependable did these options begin to surface automatically.

FIGURE 11.6
Older iterations of the Expedia date picker featured an explicit action to bring up a calendar overlay.

The calendar overlays we've seen so far don't require people's undivided attention. But when additional inputs need to be considered in isolation, a modal overlay window might be required. In this solution, the rest of the form can, in essence, be disabled so that only the additional input fields can be changed.

Naturally, let's illustrate this with an example. On the Renkoo profile form in Figure 11.7, advanced notification options are available to the frequent users who require them. The majority of people who don't need this level of control are able to simply select a single way to receive notifications. In other words, the additional inputs don't interfere with the most common ones.

When additional inputs are activated, a modal dialog window appears that allows people to specify detailed notification settings. It's important that the selections made within an overlay are visible on the original form once the overlay is closed. In the case of the calendar widget, we placed a date into the appropriate input field. In the Renkoo example in Figure 11.7, the notification settings people select are listed on the form when the modal overlay is closed.

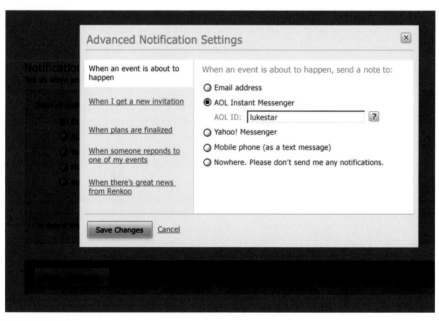

FIGURE 11.7

The advanced notification preferences on the Renkoo profile form are displayed in a modal dialog window.

If, upon seeing the additional input fields in a modal overlay, people don't want to make any additional choices, they can simply close the window using the icon in the upper-right of the dialog, cancel their selections using the Cancel link, or click anywhere off the modal overlay to return to the form.

eBay's selling form in Figure 11.8 uses a similar interaction. More savvy sellers can choose to customize the form to include options they frequently use and remove the options they don't. A modal dialog window provides these sellers with a way to pick the options they want to see on the form.

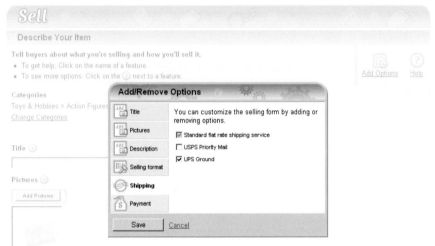

FIGURE 11.8
A modal overlay in eBay's "Sell your Item" form lets people add or remove questions on the form.

Perspective: Jack Moffett
Interaction Designer, Inmedius Inc.
Adjunct Professor, West Virginia University

A Case Study of Explosive Ordnance Disposal

It's not every day that you design a form used as the precursor to a life-and-death situation. When "Number of Deaths" is one of the field labels, you can be certain that every design decision is an important one.

Explosive Ordnance Disposal (EOD) units of the U.S. military spend a lot of effort collecting and analyzing incident data. By analyzing bomb components, incident locations, enemy tactics, and mission performance, they can improve their own tactics and procedures and better train the warfighters. Such data is collected using the EOD Incident Report, which is a massive collection of forms covering all stages of a mission.

A threat is phoned into an EOD unit, usually by local law enforcement. The warfighter taking the call must question the caller to acquire the necessary information. The interview must be thorough, but must also be completed quickly so that the mission can be planned and the team can get underway. The Initial Incident Questionnaire (IIQ) has sections for contact information, threat classification, and information about the explosive device.

One particularly complex piece of information is the threat location. There are four different formats by which the location could be reported or entered. For missions within the United States, a street address is the most likely. Tasking in combat situations will include the location in Military Grid Reference System (MGRS) format. Warfighters are accustomed to working with latitude and longitude coordinates in both decimal degrees and degrees/minutes/seconds. Regardless of the format in which it is reported and entered, the final report must use MGRS. To include all of these methods directly in the form would add a lot of complexity, presenting more opportunity for confusion and making the form too long to fit on the screen without scrolling. To keep the form as clear as possible, the location entry options were moved into a dialog accessed from a button in the IIQ.

The Location dialog provides a tab for each of the location entry methods. Any data entered in one tab will be converted or copied to the others. For example, if the warfighter were to enter a location in lat/lon coordinates and then switch to the MGRS tab, the coordinates would be converted to an MGRS value. The Address tab provides lookup

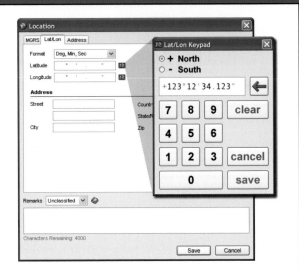

capabilities similar to mapping applications like Google Maps, from which coordinates can be derived using a geocoder. Address information may be entered in any tab, as it may be desirable alongside MGRS coordinates. When the entered location data is saved, the dialog closes. The MGRS value and any entered address information or remarks are displayed in the IIQ as an uneditable readout.

Coordinate entry is itself a significant issue. The Location dialog is used throughout the EOD Incident Report—anywhere that a location needs to be recorded. The warfighter entering the location will not always be sitting at a desk, and will therefore be using a tablet with a touch-screen. To facilitate easy entry using a finger or stylus, fields are accompanied by icons that pop up specific keypads. For example, on the Lat/Lon tab, the icon beside the Latitude and Longitude fields opens the Lat/Lon Keypad. Radio buttons allow selection of East or West (or North and South). The field in the keypad, as in the dialog, is formatted for either decimal degrees, or degrees, minutes, and seconds, depending on the selected format. It will only accept valid values. Buttons are large enough to be targeted easily by a finger. Keyboard input is also accepted, but

Perspective: Jack Moffett (Continued)

observations of warfighters indicate that they prefer to use the keypads for numerical entry even while seated and utilizing the physical keyboard.

The design of the IIQ decreases the amount of time it takes for a team to receive tasking, while at the same time improving the validity of entered data. Keypads make it easy to enter data with a finger and validate the data as it is entered. The use of dialogs with simplified readouts saves space and keeps the form readable while retaining the flexibility afforded by providing multiple entry options. In the case of this form, eliminating errors and saving time can save lives.

Progressive Engagement

Occasionally, additional inputs can be utilized to expose a set of options in a more engaging way than a typical set of input fields might. For instance, if you need your customers to select a category for their event from a list of a dozen or more potential options, a common solution would be to place the options into a single drop-down menu or perhaps several columns of radio buttons. In fact, the popular video site YouTube has used both solutions (Figure 11.9) when asking people to select a category for their videos.

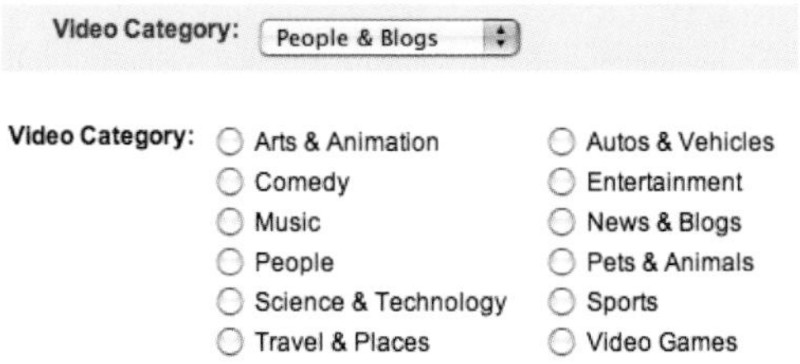

FIGURE 11.9
Two ways of selecting a category for your video on YouTube.

Contrast both of these solutions to the process of picking a category for an event on Renkoo in Figure 11.10. The initial state of this input is very approachable: a single call to action labeled "select a category." Clicking on this link exposes a colorful set of options. Selecting one of these top-level categories exposes the next level of options. Through a few seemingly innocuous clicks, people have navigated through over 30 category options, yet the process seemed kind of fun.

FIGURE 11.10
A fun category selector on Renkoo.

One of the drawbacks of this solution, however, is that all 30 options are never shown at once so people don't have the ability to see all possible choices without clicking through each of the top-level categories—perhaps an efficiency versus engagement trade-off. Another efficiency stumbling point is that the number of clicks required to pick a category is higher than the single click you'd need to pick from a set of radio buttons. Still, when a unique engagement style is more important than pure efficiency, a solution like Renkoo's might be a good fit.

Best Practices

- Additional inputs can be used to provide added or advanced options to the people who need them without getting in the way of people who don't.

- You should map additional inputs to prioritized customer needs. Primary use cases should be up front and visible; secondary use cases may be a click away.

- Additional inputs are usually more welcome when invoked by people (user-activated) than when automatically surfaced.

- Ensure that the actions that trigger additional options are clearly worded. If additional options are triggered automatically, try to provide a clue (icon, text) that sets expectations.

- Within a single form, try to maintain a consistent approach to additional inputs.

- If you need to expose a large number of additional inputs, consider using an overlay instead of exposing them inline to avoid page jumping and disorientation.

- Ensure that overlays don't cover the input fields they are helping people fill in so people can still enter an answer on their own.

- When additional options need to be considered in isolation, consider using a modal overlay.

- Make sure that there are clear ways to close or cancel a modal overlay and return to the form.

- Show the choices made in additional input overlays to people when they return to the form.

- When your primary goal is to engage customers, additional inputs can be a captivating way to step people through choices.

Selection-Dependent Inputs

Whereas flexible inputs allow people to answer questions how they want, and additional inputs allow people to include supplementary questions they want to answer, selection-dependent inputs require people to answer follow-up questions based on their answer to an initial question—usually without having to go to another Web page.

If that sounds like a mouthful, consider the following example in Figure 12.1, on the Found Bin. People have two initial options: either they are a new user or a returning user. Depending on how they answer the question, a series of follow-up questions needs to be answered. Which input fields are shown depends on the initial selection they make—hence the name, selection dependent inputs.

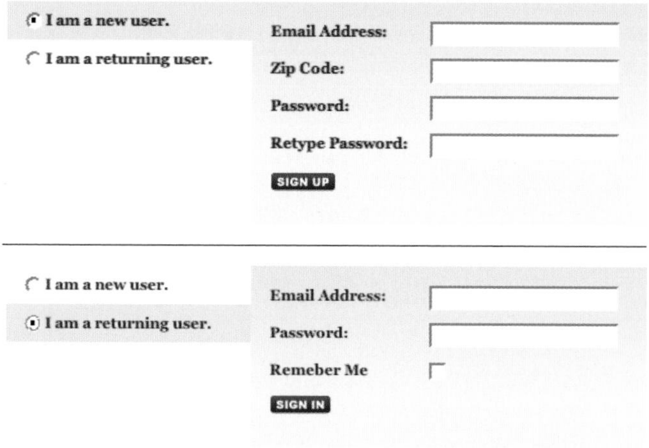

FIGURE 12.1
A simple selection-dependent input on Found Bin displays follow-up questions based on someone's initial selection.

The number of inputs that are required after an initial selection depends on the question asked. On Found Bin only a few input fields change. On the eBay download request form in Figure 12.2, lots of questions are dependent on a person's initial choice.

After an eBay seller selects the Sold option in the Listings and Records drop-down list, the form presents additional input fields for selecting a date range. Were the seller to select a different option in the Listings and Records list, completing the form would require a different set of additional options.

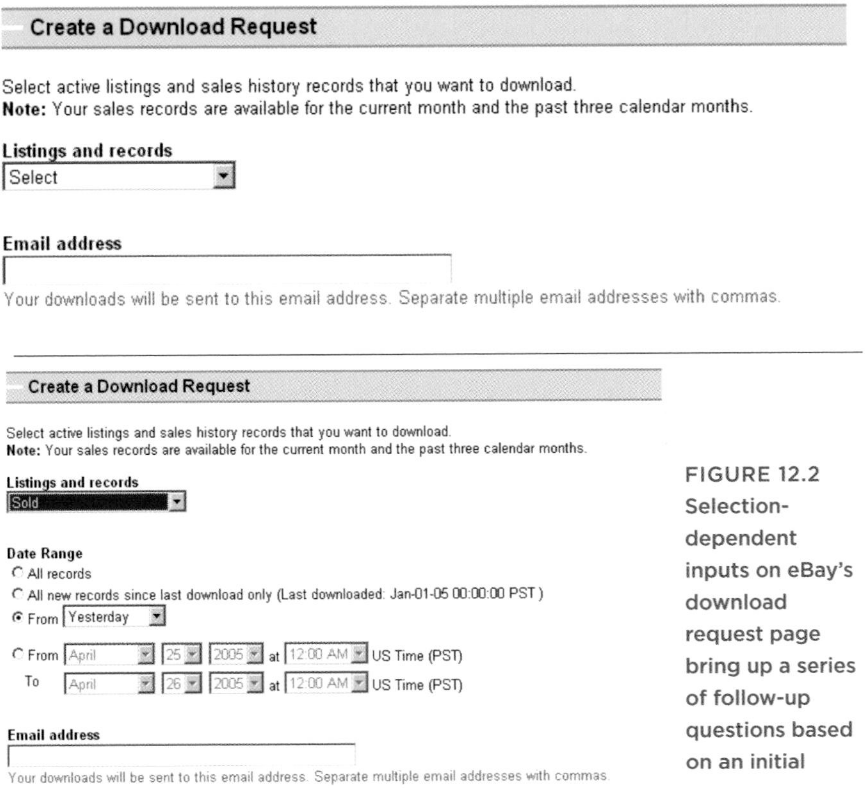

Create a Download Request

Select active listings and sales history records that you want to download.
Note: Your sales records are available for the current month and the past three calendar months.

Listings and records
Select

Email address

Your downloads will be sent to this email address. Separate multiple email addresses with commas.

Create a Download Request

Select active listings and sales history records that you want to download.
Note: Your sales records are available for the current month and the past three calendar months.

Listings and records
Sold

Date Range
- All records
- All new records since last download only (Last downloaded: Jan-01-05 00:00:00 PST)
- From Yesterday
- From April 25 2005 at 12:00 AM US Time (PST)
  To April 26 2005 at 12:00 AM US Time (PST)

Email address

Your downloads will be sent to this email address. Separate multiple email addresses with commas

FIGURE 12.2

Selection-dependent inputs on eBay's download request page bring up a series of follow-up questions based on an initial response.

It's worth pointing out that, in most cases, people cannot submit a form with selection-dependent inputs until they fill in the additional fields. In other words, selection-dependent inputs introduce additional requirements to forms.

Though both the eBay and Found Bin forms make use of selection-dependent inputs, they do so in different ways. Found Bin uses a set of vertical tabs enforced by radio buttons to present its initial options and then highlights the dependent inputs to the right of these choices. On its Create Download Request Form, eBay uses a single drop-down menu for the initial choice and then appends dependent inputs directly below this initial selection.

While selection-dependent inputs may seem like a basic user interface design problem, there are myriad solutions to be found addressing this problem online, indicating there's more complexity to this interaction than one might initially assume. In fact, each solution for selection-dependent inputs tends to have both clear advantages and disadvantages. But rather than sending you off into form land to fend for yourself, London-based usability firm Etre and I ran a series of studies testing a series of eight different selection-dependent input solutions.

As in our primary and secondary actions study outlined earlier in the book, we tested these variations on 23 people using eye-tracking and usability metrics. Participants were presented each of the eight designs in random order (to minimize familiarity biases) and asked to "Please complete the form fully and accurately." The solutions we tested were based on a list I had published online, so not every possible solution was tested. Sorry if I missed your favorite!

Page-Level Selection

Perhaps the simplest way to address selection-dependent inputs within a form is to divide the process into two clearly defined steps. On the Web, this most often translates to two separate Web pages (see Figure 12.3). The first page—or step in the process—presents people with an initial set of options. After they select one of the options, the appropriate set of selection-dependent inputs replaces their initial selection.

While the relationship between their initial selection and the dependent inputs is clear to most people, the two-step model removes valuable context (you can no longer see and easily access the options you did not choose) once users make an initial selection. This solution is also likely to be slower to complete than inline solutions that don't move between Web pages.

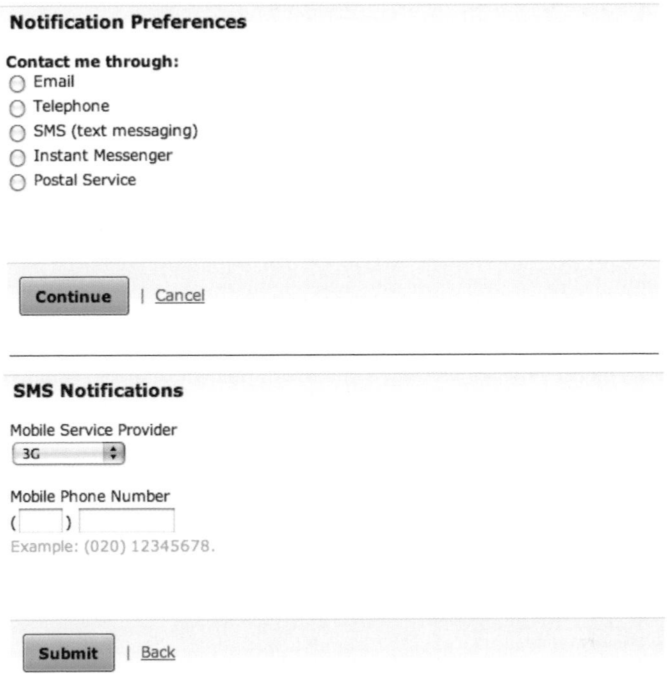

Notification Preferences

Contact me through:
○ Email
○ Telephone
○ SMS (text messaging)
○ Instant Messenger
○ Postal Service

[**Continue**] | Cancel

SMS Notifications

Mobile Service Provider
[3G ▼]

Mobile Phone Number
(____) [_____]
Example: (020) 12345678.

[**Submit**] | Back

FIGURE 12.3
Page level selection-dependent inputs place follow-up questions on a separate Web page from the initial choice.

In our testing, page-level selection performed averagely. It achieved average satisfaction scores, a relatively low number of errors, and faired well on eye-tracking measures like number of eye fixations, total length of fixations, and average fixation length. However, this solution had the second longest completion time of all the options we tested. So if you are looking for a safe solution with average performance, and quick completion times are not a concern, page-level selection-dependent inputs might be a good match.

Horizontal Tabs

To avoid additional Web pages within forms, designers have explored several inline approaches to exposing selection-dependent inputs. In one approach, horizontal tabs arranged across the top of a panel, as shown in Figure 12.4, allow people to navigate to a section of the form that contains appropriate selection-dependent inputs. The tabs present not only the initial set of options, but also provide a strong indicator of the current selection.

While most people are familiar with the concept of navigation tabs on the Web, the way in which they fill in Web forms may impair the effectiveness of this approach. When completing a form, many people move from top to bottom and, as a result, may ignore horizontal options. There may also be a lack of clarity about whether horizontal tabs are mutually exclusive. Will I submit my selections on all three tabs with the form or only the selections I made on the active tab?

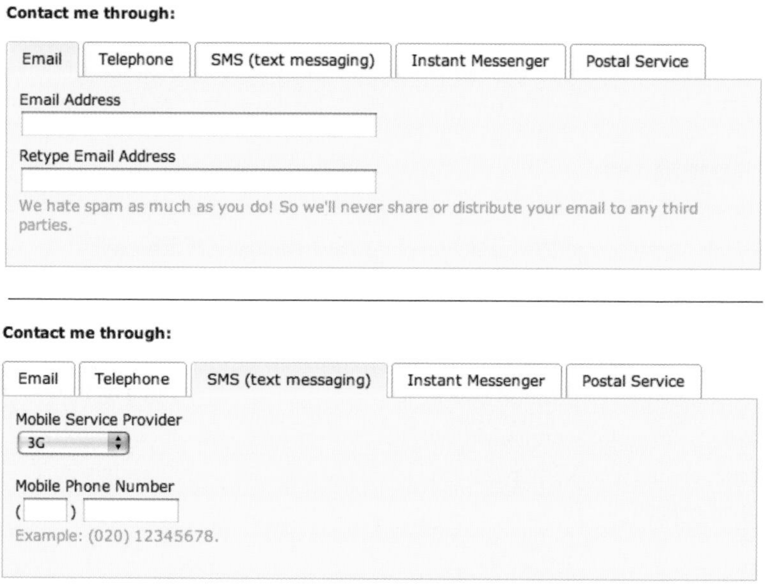

Contact me through:

| Email | Telephone | SMS (text messaging) | Instant Messenger | Postal Service |

Email Address

Retype Email Address

We hate spam as much as you do! So we'll never share or distribute your email to any third parties.

Contact me through:

| Email | Telephone | SMS (text messaging) | Instant Messenger | Postal Service |

Mobile Service Provider

3G

Mobile Phone Number

( )

Example: (020) 12345678.

FIGURE 12.4

Horizontal tab selection-dependent inputs reveal follow-up questions when people click on each tab.

If we take only standard usability metrics into account, horizontal tabs performed best overall in our testing. None of our participants made any errors, they were able to complete the task quite quickly, and they provided high satisfaction scores for this design.

However, our eye-tracking data indicated that other designs were easier to process. This may have been due to the extra effort involved in scanning across the page to read the tabs. In most of the other designs, our participants' eyes were rarely required to deviate from the left of the screen to the right. Horizontal tabs clearly deviated from a clear scan line to completion (see Figure 12.5).

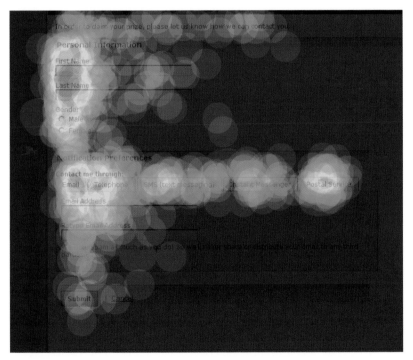

FIGURE 12.5
A heat map of people's eye fixations on horizontal tab selection-dependent inputs reveals how this form is parsed visually. Image provided by Etre.

One issue that did not come up in our testing of horizontal tabs but that I have seen in other usability studies was confusion over whether or not people's inputs in each of the tabs were mutually exclusive. Perhaps the strong visual indicator of which tab was active helped alleviate these anxieties and make it clearer that only the active tab's contents would be submitted.

Vertical Tabs

To compensate for the potential lack of visibility of horizontal tabs when people move from top to bottom through a form, vertically stacked tabs, as seen in Figure 12.6, are intended to be positioned directly within people's scan line.

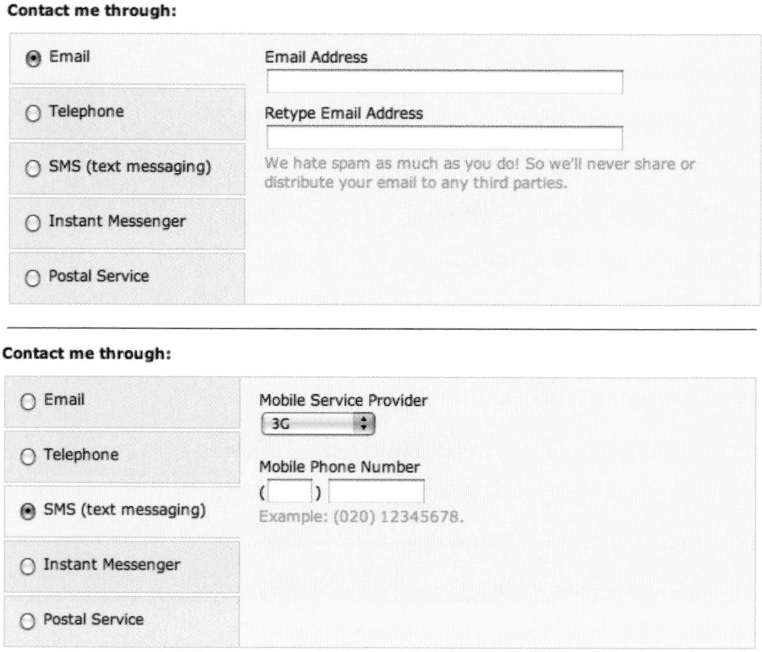

FIGURE 12.6
Vertical tab selection-dependent inputs reveal follow-up questions to the right of an initial selection.

In terms of ease on the eye, vertical tabs performed best in our testing. This solution had the lowest total length of eye fixations, the lowest average fixation length, and one of the lowest average number of fixations.

Like two other solutions we tested, vertical tabs hid irrelevant form controls from people until they needed them. This factor seems to have been critical for ease on the eye and for the speed with which our participants were able to complete the forms. (The same three solutions also had the three lowest average completion times.)

Along with two other solutions we tested, vertical tabs also achieved near-perfect satisfaction ratings. These scores may result from the fact that the three solutions all display radio buttons and their selection-dependent inputs in close proximity to one another. This ensures that someone's eye doesn't have to travel too far (Figure 12.7) once a radio button has been selected, making the design more efficient.

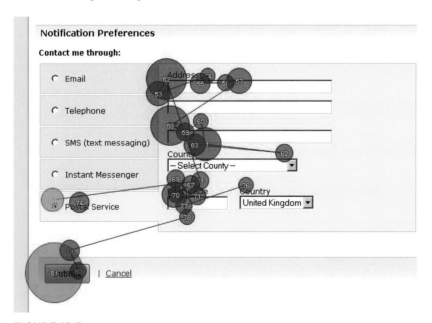

FIGURE 12.7
People's eyes don't have to travel far between initial options and additional inputs in vertical tab selection-dependent inputs. Image provided by Etre.

Despite all this good news, a couple people made mistakes using this design and were a little confused as to whether the vertical tabs were mutually exclusive or not. Interestingly, people seemed less confused by the horizontal tabs, which theoretically should have bred more confusion because they break with desktop application conventions where most horizontal tabs are not mutually exclusive. The vertical tabs design also included radio buttons on each tab to help to communicate that they were mutually exclusive options.

In other usability testing I have seen, vertical tabs have out performed horizontal tabs for these very reasons. And since vertical tabs score better on satisfaction, eye-tracking metrics, and time to completion, my inclination is to prefer them to horizontal tabs.

Drop-Down List

Both the horizontal and vertical tab solutions maintain a unique interface element—in this case, a tab—for each initial option. This keeps all the initial options visible, but also requires considerable screen real estate to do so. When the number of initial options grows, these methods tend not to scale very well.

The drop-down list solution shown in Figure 12.8 utilizes a menu and grouping box to confine all selection-dependent inputs to a specific area of the form. Though this method obscures most of the initial options—as only one option is visible in the drop-down list at a time—using a single control may better communicate the scope and impact of the initial selection.

FIGURE 12.8
Drop-down list selection-dependent inputs allow people to select follow-up questions from a potentially long list of initial options without requiring a lot of screen real estate.

Contact me through:

SMS (text messaging)

Mobile Service Provider
3G

Mobile Phone Number
(   )
Example: (020) 12345678

Like vertical tabs, the drop-down list solution hid irrelevant form inputs from people until they needed them. This meant drop-down list selection-dependent inputs were easy on the eyes and completed quite quickly. On the other data points we measured, the drop-down list solution performed average with relatively high satisfaction scores and only a single error made by 23 participants.

As a result, drop-down list selection-dependent inputs are likely a safe way to go when your list of initial options scales past a number that either horizontal or vertical tabs can support.

Expose Below Radio Buttons

Another inline solution for selection-dependent inputs involves vertically separating the initial options from their respective additional inputs. This approach, shown in Figure 12.9, has the advantage of always keeping all the initial options—and a person's selection among those options—visible.

A strong visual indication of the dependency between the initial selection and its additional inputs can help communicate their relationship more clearly.

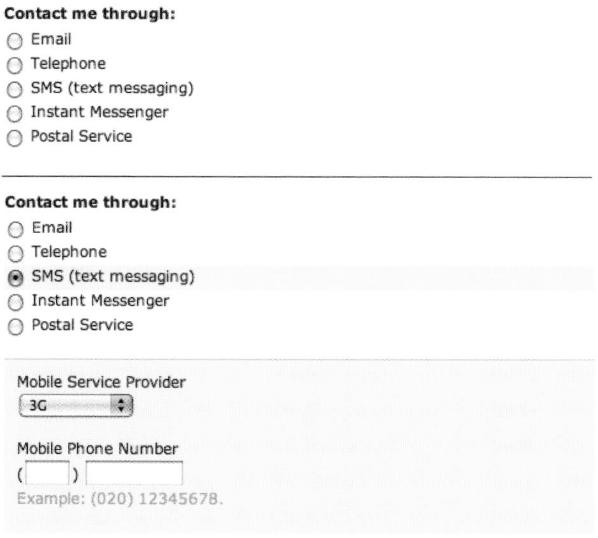

Contact me through:
- ◯ Email
- ◯ Telephone
- ◯ SMS (text messaging)
- ◯ Instant Messenger
- ◯ Postal Service

Contact me through:
- ◯ Email
- ◯ Telephone
- ◉ SMS (text messaging)
- ◯ Instant Messenger
- ◯ Postal Service

Mobile Service Provider
[3G ▼]

Mobile Phone Number
(___) [_____]
Example: (020) 12345678.

FIGURE 12.9
Exposed below selection-dependent inputs surface follow-up questions in a consistent location below an initial set of questions.

However, the jumping effect that occurs when people change their selections and the screen updates to show a revised set of additional inputs can potentially disorientate people especially when the set of additional inputs is long.

Like vertical tabs, this solution also achieved near-perfect satisfaction ratings likely stemming from the fact that it displays radio buttons and their selection-dependent inputs in close proximity to one another.

However, in hindsight, this solution wasn't tested as well as it might have been. As part of their task, we asked participants to select Postal Service: the last radio button in the group. As a result, the additional inputs appeared directly below the active radio button. This solution is likely to have performed worse if we had asked for a different option because the visual separation of the selected radio button and its related form options would likely have caused more visual discomfort for people.

In other testing I've observed, this has been the case. After trying a few different options in the initial set of radio buttons, people lose sight of which option is active and its relationship to the selection-dependent inputs. This phenomenon becomes even more problematic when the quantity of selection-dependent options is large because the association between the initial selection and additional options becomes less clear.

Expose Within Radio Buttons

Similar to the expose below solution, the expose within solution reveals additional inputs within a set of initial options, as shown in Figure 12.10. When the set of additional inputs is quite small—one to two additional inputs—this method can maintain the context of a person's initial selection while introducing the required selection-dependent inputs where they are most relevant.

Because this solution displayed radio buttons and their selection-dependent inputs in very close proximity to one another, it also achieved near-perfect satisfaction ratings. The "expose within radio buttons" method also hid irrelevant form inputs from people until they needed them. This meant

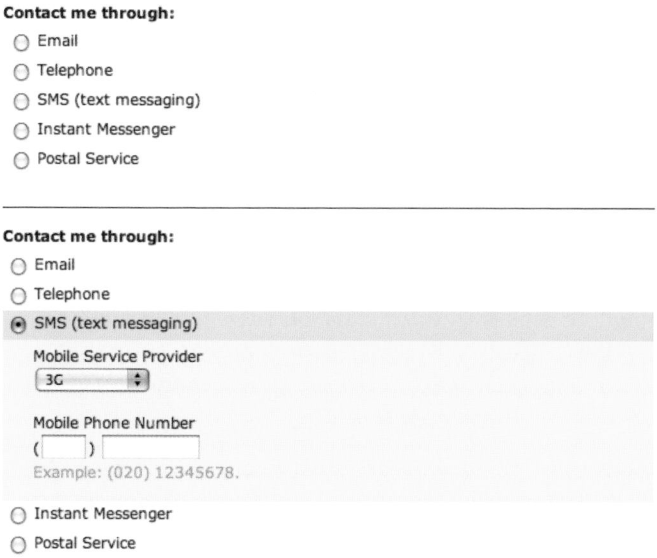

Contact me through:

○ Email
○ Telephone
○ SMS (text messaging)
○ Instant Messenger
○ Postal Service

Contact me through:

○ Email
○ Telephone
◉ SMS (text messaging)

    Mobile Service Provider
    [3G   ◆]

    Mobile Phone Number
    (   ) [   ]
    Example: (020) 12345678.

○ Instant Messenger
○ Postal Service

FIGURE 12.10
Exposed within selection-dependent inputs surface follow-up questions directly below each initial choice.

it was easy on the eyes and completed quite quickly. In fact, this was the fastest solution we tested and had the lowest number of average fixations.

However, a couple of people made errors while completing the task, and similar concerns apply here as with the exposed below radio button solution. If the number of selection-dependent inputs is substantial, this method breaks down quickly. The combination of page jumping and the movement of the initial set of options—as the elements between them are revealed and hidden—makes for a disorientating interaction that frequently has people questioning which user interface element triggers which set of options.

As a result, a clear visual association between initial selection and additional options is even more important, since we don't want people losing sight of their top-level selection. A small number of selection-dependent inputs and animated transitions when people change their initial selections also help make this method work.

Exposed Inactive

To address the disorientation caused by the movement of initial selection options when a person jumps between them, the exposed, but inactive solution shown in Figure 12.11 keeps all additional inputs visible, but makes only one set of options available at a time. The other selection-dependent inputs are unavailable and thus most commonly appear dimmed, or grayed out.

While this method does keep all additional inputs visible and within the context of an initial selection, the sheer volume of inputs that are visible quickly overwhelms people. Also, when there are many additional inputs

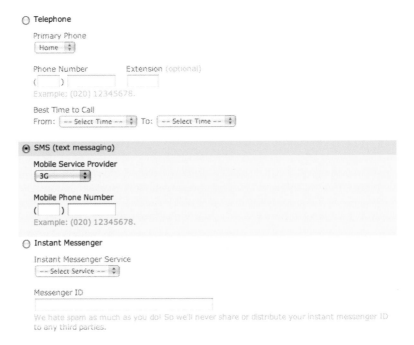

FIGURE 12.11

Exposed inactive selection-dependent inputs show all follow-up questions in an inactive state when not selected.

for each initial option, the association between the person's selection and the other initial options gets lost. Adding to this effect is the fact that the visible difference between inactive and active elements is frequently too subtle for people to notice.

This solution was one of the least-liked and worst performing we tested. In fact, it had the longest completion times of any option tested. Participants were displeased with the sheer length of these pages (to put it mildly) and were annoyed at having to attend to (and subsequently dismiss) sections of the form that they didn't need to fill in.

Although this design performed quite poorly, it was superior in every metric we measured to the exposed groups solution outlined next. The only difference between these two solutions was the graying out of unused inputs, so we can pretty confidently conclude the graying out of irrelevant options improved the design. Of course, since the two exposed options were our worst performing, we can also conclude that hiding form options when they are not required is an even better solution.

Exposed Groups

To compensate for the disassociation between the set of initial options in the exposed inactive method, the example in Figure 12.12 uses visual groupings to bind each set of selection-dependent inputs beneath an initial selection.

In this method, however, the visual weight of the many additional inputs quickly reduces the visibility of the initial set of options.

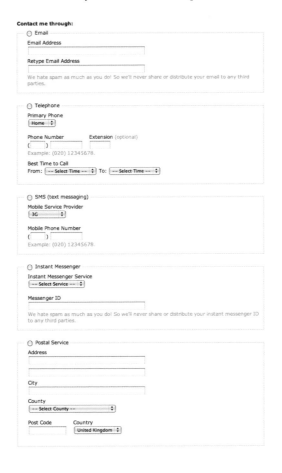

FIGURE 12.12
Exposed groups of selection-dependent inputs show all follow-up questions in addition to an initial set of choices.

This option had the lowest success rate, highest number of errors made, and lowest satisfaction of all the solutions we tested. Our eye-tracking data revealed that participants made a whopping 18 more fixations when using the exposed groups solution than they did using the inline exposure solution (see Figure 12.13).

Due to the excessive problems found with this solution, I think it is a safe bet to avoid it.

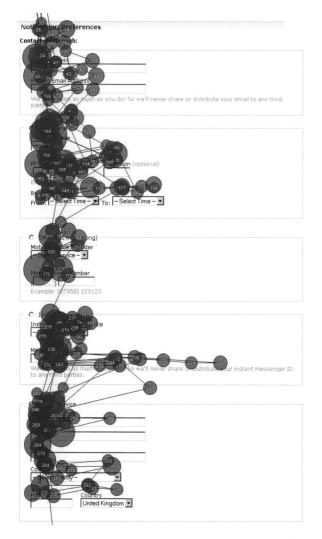

FIGURE 12.13
Exposed groups of selection-dependent inputs resulted in a lot of eye fixations. Image provided by Etre.

Best Practices

Well, I warned you that selection-dependent inputs have lots of considerations, didn't I? Now that we're through that deluge of data, what have we learned?

- Page-level selection-dependent inputs are probably your best bet when the number of additional options for each initial choice is large. Though you need two Web pages to break up the form, the dynamic hiding and showing of additional inputs won't confuse people, and they won't need to question whether or not their choices are mutually exclusive.

- Vertical and horizontal tabs actually perform quite well in all-around usability, satisfaction, and eye-tracking metrics but come with the gnarly problem of mutual exclusivity. I've gotten conflicting data on which of these options resolves this issue so they both seem to be stuck with it. If you can get around mutual exclusivity through clever interaction or visual design, good performance is yours to be had with these solutions.

- When you have a long list of initial options (more than 4 or 5) each with its unique set of selection-dependent inputs, using a drop-down list and visual grouping for the additional options is likely a good way to go.

- If you only have a few additional inputs for each initial option, exposed below radio buttons or exposed within radio buttons might be your best option. I've seen both of these options cause confusion with excessive page jumping and disassociation between initial choices, so tread carefully. But if you really only have 1–3 additional fields per initial choice, I'd go with exposed inline radio buttons. Just make sure you use clear visual associations and transitions, if possible.

- All options exposed as inactive or all options exposed are basically nonstarters because people are quickly overwhelmed by too many options that don't map to their goals.

- Overall, hiding irrelevant form controls from people until they need them results in forms that are easy on the eyes and completed quite quickly.

Best Practices (Continued)

- Overall, displaying initial options and their selection-dependent inputs in close proximity to one another seems to lead to high satisfaction ratings.

- In all cases, maintain a clear association between the initial selection options. Don't let people lose sight of their initial top-level choice.

- In all cases, clearly associate selection-dependent inputs with their trigger. All the examples outlined in this section do so with either yellow backgrounds or gray outlines.

- In all cases, avoid excessive page jumping that disassociates selection-dependent inputs from the initial set of options.

Gradual
Engagement

I'll just come out and say this: sign-up forms must die. In the introduction to this book I described the process of stumbling upon or being recommended a Web service. You arrive eager to dive in and start engaging and what's the first thing that greets you? A form.

We can do better. In fact, I believe we can get people engaged with digital services in a way that tells them how they work and why they should care enough to use them.[1] I also believe we can do this without explicitly making them fill out a sign-up form as a first step.

Signing Up

But before we get into the potential of gradual engagement (your path out of sign-in "dullery"), let's look at how the process of engaging with an online service typically works. Since 2007 was a breakout year for online video, it's safe to assume a lot of people went on the Web to post one of their videos. Perhaps they heard Google Video was a good place to do so. Upon arriving at the site, they found a link to share their video and what happened next? They got the form in Figure 13.1.

You are required to give us your email address, select a password, tell us your name, your location, verify this strange word, agree to our terms of service, and finally, you will get what's behind the form.

---

[1] For more about encouraging people to try Web applications through the sign-up process, check out Joshua Porter's book: *Designing for the Social Web*, New Riders, 2008.

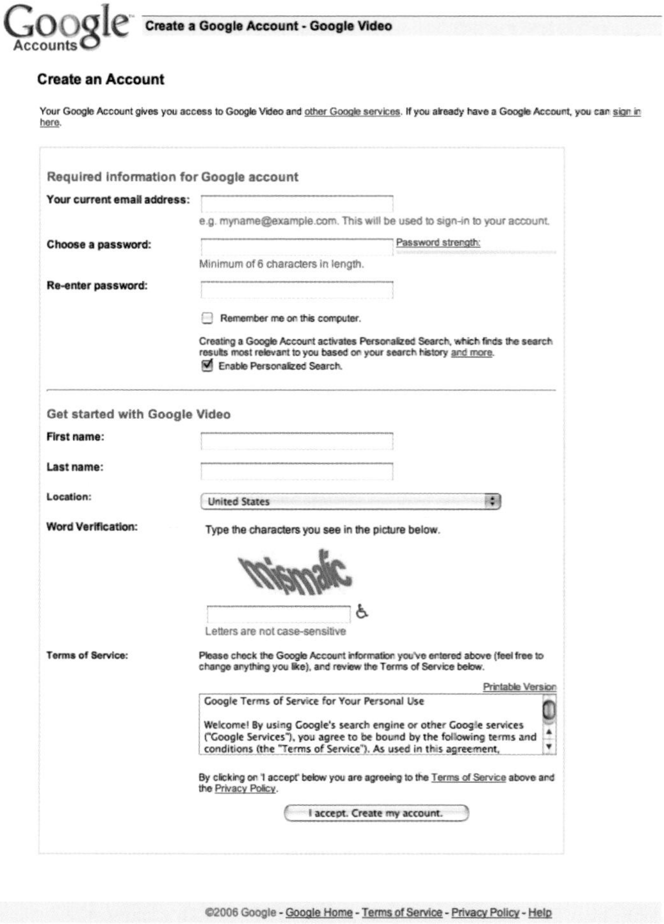

FIGURE 13.1
A sign-up form greets new customers at Google Video.

Getting Engaged

Now contrast this approach with that of another online video service: Jumpcut. The primary calls to action on the Jumpcut front page, as seen in Figure 13.2, are Make a Movie and Try a Demo. Right out of the gates, Jumpcut is interested in telling you how its service works and why it's great for you. So let's dive in.

FIGURE 13.2
The process
of adding
a video to
Jumpcut
introduces
you to the
services the
site provides,
namely
online video
editing.

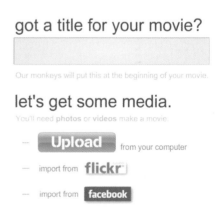

jumpcut™

Home   Your Page   Explore   Create   Upload   Groups

Upload video, photos, music

Upload

Winner
Best Upload Ever
2006 - Upload Festival

import from flickr or facebook   any questions ❓

---

jumpcut™

Help | Register | Sign In

Home   Your Page   Explore   Create   Upload   Groups

Pick a Style:

○ None
○ Smooth
○ Net Love
○ Quiet
○ Time Reversal
○ Wild
○ The Jumpcut
○ Speed Up

⟳ **Edit My Movie** ❓

🟣 **Publish My Movie** ❓

DSC05766anx

import from flickr or facebook   Upload More   any questions ❓

Selecting Make a Movie brings up a single input field for the title of your movie and a few options you can use to upload media files for your movie. Selecting Upload from this list allows you to add images, audio, and video from your desktop computer. Once you do, you are put in Jumpcut's Web-based video editor. Here you can edit your movie; add styles; coordinate your audio, video, and images, and more.

So far, no sign-up form. It's only when you want to publish or share your movie that Jumpcut asks for your name and email so you and others can access the movie you just made. Through this process, you learned what Jumpcut does, and you did it without having to jump through a sign-up form. That's gradual engagement.

Let's look at another example. Geni is a Web service that allows anyone to set up a family tree and share it with family and friends. What's the first thing potential customers need to do when they arrive at Geni? Fill out a registration form? Nope, they make a family tree. After all, that's what's Geni is for.

The front page of Geni (Figure 13.3) makes it clear what the site is for. So get started creating a family tree by entering your name and email address. Next, you can add your parents, their siblings, or your siblings—in no time, you have a pretty good family tree going. While you were at it, Geni sent you an email with your username and password so you can get back to your family tree anytime you want.

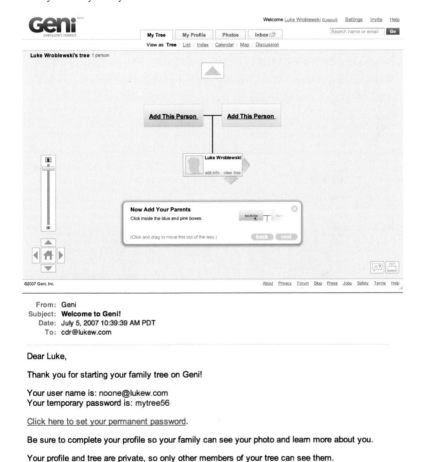

FIGURE 13.3

Geni's process of creating a family tree contains no explicit registration forms and gets people acquainted with Geni's service right away.

Once again through the process of gradual engagement, you learned what a Web service does, and you did it without an explicit registration form requiring you to fork over a lot of information. In Geni's case, the approach to gradual engagement has given the service five million profiles in five months. Not too shabby.

It's worth noting that any Web service that automatically sets up an account for its customers may leave some people confused about whether they actually have an account or not. After all, they did not explicitly create one. As a result, these services need to ensure they have an easy way for people to access their account information if they did not see or chose to ignore the email they were sent outlining their account information.

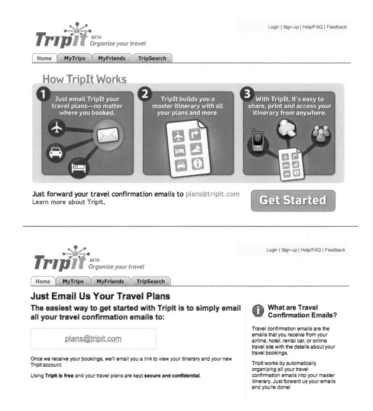

Another example of gradual engagement comes from TripIt: a Web service that allows people to assemble a trip itinerary, complete with weather and driving directions, using only their flight, hotel, and rental car confirmation emails. The first step to getting started is emailing TripIt a confirmation email from upcoming or past travel. TripIt will send you back a note that provides access to an automatically created personal travel itinerary (see Figure 13.4).

FIGURE 13.4
Using TripIt starts by forwarding a travel confirmation email—not with a sign-up form.

Once again, your first step in using TripIt is not a sign-up form. Instead, you learn how the service works by actually using it. TripIt gets your name and email address from the confirmation emails you send the service. From there, if you want to edit your name, email, or create a password to access the site, you can do so. Chances are you will do so now that you know how the service works and how it benefits you.

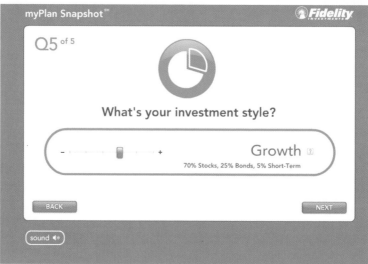

When you're exploring if gradual engagement might be right for your Web service, it's important to consider how a series of interactions can explain how potential customers can use your service and why they should care. Gradual engagement isn't well served by simply distributing each of your sign-up form input fields onto separate Web pages.

While I applaud Fidelity's myplan form (Figure 13.5) for its attempt at making financial planning more enjoyable, I'm not sure distributing each of its input fields to separate Web pages and presenting them as slider inputs is the best way to achieve the goal of getting people to understand what Fidelity can do for them.

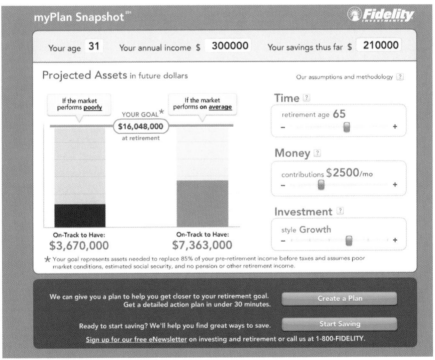

FIGURE 13.5
Fidelity's myplan form divides a series of input into stand-alone slider interactions.

Best Practices

- When planning a customer's initial experience for your Web service, think about how you can avoid sign-up forms in favor of gradual engagement.

- If you do opt for a gradual engagement solution, ensure that it gives potential customers an understanding of how they can use your service and why they should care.

- If you choose to auto-generate accounts for potential customers, ensure there is a clear way for them to access their account. Chances are that people will either ignore or not see account creation emails, and may be uncertain if they have an account or not.

- Avoid gradual engagement solutions that simply distribute the various input fields in a sign-up form across multiple pages. It's a good possibility that this will reduce efficiency and not delight anyone.

CHAPTER 14

What's Next?

As crucial components of ecommerce, online communication, and Web applications, Web forms aren't going anywhere just yet. Though as I hope you've seen in this book, there's lots of room for improvement in how we design and manage forms online. As we move forward, there are even more ways we could do better still.

The Disappearing Form

In Chapter 13, I walked through a number of examples of forms with gradual engagement. As people interacted with sites that followed these principles, chances are they didn't even realize they were filling in a form. Instead, they felt they were making a movie or setting up a family tree. Gradual engagements like these have the potential to make forms essentially disappear by focusing on the things people want to achieve instead of the data fields required by a back-end database. That's our friend the "outside in" instead of "inside out" way of thinking.

Another way for forms to fade toward invisibility is through dynamic or game-like interactions. As an example, Uzanto's Mind Canvas[1] software (Figure 14.1) uses *game-like elicitation methods (GEMs)* to make the data

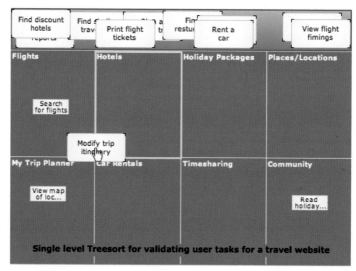

FIGURE 14.1
Game-like elicitation methods in the Mind Canvas research tool.

---

[1] http://www.themindcanvas.com/

collection process a more fun and engaging experience. People who used Mind Canvas to participate in market research have raved about the level of enjoyment they had when "filling out a survey."

In addition to interactions like these, technology solutions may also help to push some forms behind the scenes. Systems like Microsoft's Live ID[2] (formerly know as *Microsoft Passport*) and the open source project OpenID[3] are single sign-in solutions that allow people to use multiple Web sites with only one account. Although these approaches have the potential to eliminate a lot of duplicative sign-up and checkout forms online, neither has become a clear standard just yet.

The Changing Form

In situations where forms aren't likely to disappear anytime soon, they may want to start changing. The principles I described for personalized defaults in Chapter 10 could ultimately be used to determine how forms should be different for specific individuals. Know someone is likely to type in a long comment? Provide a large text area to do so. Is a different person likely to be extremely terse with his comments? Perhaps, he only requires two lines of input to respond.

---

[2] http://en.wikipedia.org/wiki/Windows_Live_ID

[3] http://www.openid.net

Before anyone starts coding forms that change based on who's using them, it's important to note that adaptive interfaces like these are prone to cause confusion when not designed well. If you've ever used a Microsoft Office menu (Figure 14.2) and wondered where an option you saw before has gone, you've encountered the negative side of "adaptive interfaces." In a nutshell, when adaptive interfaces work well[4], they provide a slightly better experience for a few people. When they don't work well, they can provide a lot of confusion for many people.

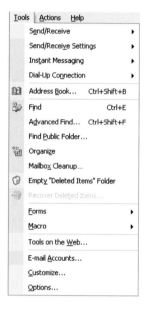

FIGURE 14.2
Microsoft's Office menu hides options when you don't use them frequently.

4 For more on adaptive interfaces, see Stephen Anderson's talk from IA Summit 2007: http://tinyurl.com/25akke

Perspective: Aaron Gustafson
Principal, Easy! Designs, LLC
Contributing Author: *Accelerated DOM Scripting with Ajax, APIs, and Libraries*
Member, Web Standards Project (WaSP)

Zen and the Art of HTML Forms

The only thing that could possibly be more painful than filling out a form is making one, especially in HTML. But it doesn't have to be that way. Following these three simple steps will have you loving (well, maybe that's a bit strong) your forms in no time.

STEP 1: LET THE FREAK FLAGS FLY!

HTML forms are long, tedious, and repetitive to code, but even that would be bearable if their controls rendered consistently across the different browsers and operating systems—which they don't. Form controls are the denizens of HTML's Island of Misfit Toys: a strange mix of lonely, misunderstood, and oddly put-together elements.

To truly master form construction on the Web, you'll need to get past all of that. You'll need to embrace the eccentricities of form controls, and maybe even be a little Zen-like about the strange characteristics they exhibit. After all, it's not their fault—they're just rendered that way.

STEP 2: FIND THE INNER MEANING.

At their core, form controls are just like other HTML elements and should be treated as such. Each means something different, and when combined correctly, they work together to give context and meaning to your forms. In the hands of experts, they can even tell a story.

STEP 3: BREAK DOWN THE MARKUP.

So how do you harness the untapped potential in form controls? Well, the first step is to understand what they do and don't do. Once you've got that down, it's all about figuring out how to combine them with other form controls and other bits of HTML to provide the greatest amount of meaning and context to users.

And the key to success in HTML form alchemy is breaking down complex tasks and structures into simpler ones.

PUTTING IT ALL TOGETHER

Consider a long form composed of multiple-choice questions. If you begin breaking that down, you might recognize the form as a list of questions. Hmm...a list:

```
<form ...>
  <ol>
    <li>What is your favorite fruit?</li>
    ...
  </ol>
</form>
```

At the next level down, you have an individual multiple-choice question. A multiple-choice question is really composed of two things: a question and a list of possible responses. You might think the question is a perfect use for the LABEL element, but that element should really be used to provide context for an individual form control. In this case, a LEGEND is more appropriate (with the entire component becoming a FIELDSET), as it is used to provide context for a group of fields:

```
...
<li>
  <fieldset>
    <legend>What is your favorite fruit?</legend>
    <ul>
      <li>strawberries</li>
      ...
    </ul>
  </fieldset>
</li>
...
```

Down another level, you'll find the possible responses. You already know that each is contained in a list item, but you also know that each is composed of two elements: a radio INPUT and some text to describe what that form control stands for, a LABEL. Marking it up is easy enough:

```
. . .
  <li><label><input type="radio" name="fruit"
value="strawberries" /> strawberries</label></li>
. . .
```

BUT WHAT ABOUT DESIGN?

Equally as important as solid markup in building successful forms is designing them. This is the bit that most Web developers hate because of the myriad of inconsistent form control implementations to deal with.

A foundation of rich, semantic markup makes form design quite easy, though. For instance, one of the most basic layouts for a form is a stacked series of labels and form controls. This is easily achieved by setting the LABEL elements to display block and creating a little extra space between the list items in your form:

```
label {
  display: block;
}
form li {
  margin-bottom: .5em;
}
```

Perspective: Aaron Gustafson (Continued)

But let's say you want to change the form to display labels and form controls side-by-side. That's equally easy:

```css
label {
   display: block;
   float: left;
   width: 40%;
}
form li {
   clear: both;
   margin-bottom: .5em;
}
```

It's all about working with the markup you have and then applying your knowledge of CSS layout to the form elements. Just be sure to keep in mind that form controls render quite differently across different browsers and operating systems, so don't spend too much time trying to achieve pixel-perfection.

Using simple techniques like these help you develop consistent, repeatable markup and design patterns that will make working with forms much more satisfying and pleasant.

Getting It Built

After you've internalized some of the best practices in this book, I hope you'll want to bring them to life on your forms. Though the code behind these solutions is beyond the scope of this book, Aaron Gustafson's perspective in this chapter should give you a nice outline for how you can approach the development of Web forms on your site.

If you'd like to get a Web form up and running quickly, several online services have great tools to help you design, build, and host many kinds of forms. Although I haven't evaluated them all, Wufoo[5] and Form Assembly[6] have stood out from the pack for me.

When you are ready to dive even deeper, the World Wide Web Consortium (W3C)'s Forms Working Group[7] is a place to learn about the next generation of forms technology for the Web. In particular, the W3C's XForms standard separates what a form does and how a form looks into distinct markup.

However you decide to develop your forms, just remember to think from the viewpoint of the people who will be using them (the outside in perspective). After all, we don't want forms to suck forever, do we?

---

5 http://wufoo.com/

6 http://www.formassembly.com/

7 http://www.w3.org/MarkUp/Forms/

Index

grouping 82, 84
help text within 109
labels within 63
lengths 73
optional 78
required 75
Tab key for moving between 52
types 68

J

Jarrett, Caroline 22, 23
Jotspot Live 130
Juicy Studios 110
   inline help system 111
Jumpcut 197

K

Kayak
   calendar overlay 164
   inline suggestions 146
keyboard
   as only access 49
   vs. mouse 51

L

LABEL element 212
   display block for 213
labels 51, 56
   alignment 56
   best practices 37, 65
   in conversation 25
   within inputs 63
   left-aligned 34
   for links 51
   mixed alignment 64
language, and label length 57
Lastfm.com, inline validation 144
layout, information conveyed by 52
left-aligned labels 34, 56, 61
legend, for symbol 78
LEGEND element 212
length of input fields 73
LinkedIn
   help text 109, 110
   success page 136

links, labels for 51
list boxes 69
lists, HTML for 212
Live ID (Microsoft) 209
Location dialog 170
login forms 16

M

Macy's
   Billing Information form 74
   required input 77
marketing
   messages 126
   opt-in for materials 101
   questions for 30
messages
   animated 135
   visual and textual framework
     for 126
Microsoft
   Live ID 209
   Office menu 210
   Passport 209
Military Grid Reference System (MGRS)
   format 169
Mind Canvas (Uzanto) 208
Mint, sign-up form 145
modal dialog window 166, 167
   for error message 123
Moffett, Jack 169
mouse, vs. keyboard 51
MovieTickets.com, drop-down
   menus 72

N

names for forms 40
networks, disabling images over slow 49
Newsvine 142
Norman, Donald, The Design of Everyday Things 73

O

"outsidein" design 2, 208
Office Depot, registration form 53
OpenID 209

ACKNOWLEDGMENTS

Though countless Web designers, developers, and their forms inspired and influenced the content in this book, there was a particular sequence of events that made the book itself possible.

Step one was the eBay Platform design team—Jamie Hoover, Micah Alpern, James Reffell, and Larry Cornett—who showed me the power of subtle design choices in Web forms. Their work and insights built the groundwork for how and why I think about form design. And three of them took their time to review this book in its early stages—thanks guys.

Step two came from Joshua Porter, Jared Spool, and Christine Perfetti at User Interface Engineering (UIE) who believed I could present a session about form design at their Web App Summit in January of 2007. This was the spark that led me to take what I knew about Web form design and turn it into something that could be shared with others.

Step three was Liz Danzico and Lou Rosenfeld at Rosenfeld Media believing that we had the makings of a book on our hands and bringing in Marta Justak and Susan Honeywell to help make it happen through top-notch editing and design. Simon Griffin, Paul Schwartfeger, Dan Griffin and colleagues at Etre Ltd. in London (www.etre.com) rounded out this fantastic team with original eye-tracking and usability research just for this book.

Along the way, the comments and questions from bloggers, conference attendees, mailing lists, fellow designers, researchers, and developers stewed big thoughts and added the insights that made this book what it is today. Although I lack the room to list everyone, I would like to highlight the work of Matteo Penzo, Caroline Jarrett, Bob Baxley, and Aaron Gustafson in spreading the good form design gospel.

Of course, none of these pieces would have fit into place if it weren't for the continual support (and patience) of my wife Amanda. Thanks for letting a Web geek type away late into the night....

ABOUT THE AUTHOR

It all started in my freshman year of college. I'd be drawing still lifes in art class in the afternoon and be holed up in the digital computer lab late at night coding my computer science homework.

That need to balance form and function has stayed with me ever since. It led me to work at the National Center for Supercomputing Applications (NCSA), where the first popular graphical Web browser, NCSA Mosaic, was born and gave rise to Web surfing. The Web took design and technology and produced experiences. I was hooked with both left and right brain.

After several years of designing Web destinations and tools at NCSA and beyond, I went on to teach classes on Interface Design at the University of Illinois' School of Library and Information Sciences. I codified my approach to teaching in my first book, *Site-Seeing: A Visual Approach to Web Usability* (John Wiley, 2002). While some Web pundits argued for a more visual Web and others stressed pure usability, I again focused on the need for balance and outlined why visual communication and usability are locked in a symbiotic dance.

In the years that followed, I spent time as the Lead User Interface Designer in eBay Inc.'s platform team, where I led the strategic design of new consumer products and internal tools and processes. I began to publish "Functioning Form," a leading online publication for Web experience design. I was a founding board member of the Interaction Design Association (IxDA), and I spoke at numerous conferences and companies around the world about Web design and strategy.

During that time and now in my current role as Senior Principal of Product Ideation & Design at Yahoo! Inc., I designed or contributed to software used by hundreds of millions of people. Underlying it all is that simple balance of function and form. It's that philosophy you'll find underlying every page in this book, and I still believe it's what ultimately makes the Web useful, usable, and enjoyable.